Previous Books by Gordon L. Weil

The European Convention on Human Rights
A Handbook on the European Economic Community
A Foreign Policy for Europe
Trade Policy in the Seventies
The Benelux Nations
The Gold War (with Ian Davidson)
The Long Shot
American Trade Policy: A New Round
The Consumer's Guide to Banks
Election '76
Sears, Roebuck, U.S.A.

THE WELFARE DEBATE
of
1978

Gordon L. Weil

With additional material by
Samuel I. Eskenazi

Foreword by
Leonard M. Greene

The Institute for
Socioeconomic Studies

White Plains, New York

The Institute for Socioeconomic Studies
Airport Road, White Plains, New York 10604

CONTENTS

FOREWORD

When President Carter submitted his Program for Better Jobs and Income to the Congress in 1977, he opened the first major debate on Capitol Hill over welfare policy since the 1969-1971 consideration of President Nixon's Family Assistance Plan. Following the Carter proposal, House and Senate committees as well as scores of interest groups joined in what became national debate of welfare reform. The present "system," the consensus had it, is a grave burden on government at every level, is abused by widespread corruption, and is dangerously corrosive of basic American values — like the work ethic.

In an earlier study, *An Inventory of Federal Income Transfer Programs, Fiscal Year 1977,* The Institute for Socioeconomic Studies published information on the profusion of overlapping, contradictory benefit programs now provided for income maintenance and to "fight poverty." The Institute's study — information not previously available to the nation — reveals that there are 182 such programs. In 1977, they involved an astounding $248.1 billion. The well-being and stability of the nation require consolidation and reduction of these programs. Although it is apparent as I write that no major legislation will emerge from the welfare debate of 1978, the Carter proposal and some of the alternatives that have come forward have had the value of prompting greater awareness of the necessary consolidation of the many programs that now make up "welfare."

The various bills put forward also inspire hope that whatever reform is ultimately enacted will coordinate the benefit reduction rates under various programs to insure that their combined impact on recipients' income is not excessive. Today, when a welfare recipient manages to earn perhaps so little as an extra dollar, this increment can send him or her past a "cutoff point." All or many of the recipient's benefits may be jeopardized. Common sense obviously conflicts with any ambition to get a job and earn money. All of this must be turned around. Every effort must be made to stimulate permanent employment in the private sector — as opposed to permanent reliance on public service employment. Toward this end, there was one welcome initiative in the 1978 debate. One proposal given substantial support would have provided the earned income tax credit only to those finding private-sector employment.

Finally, the welfare system should not encourage needless migration by offering more attractive benefits in one state than in another. The establishment of an adequate national minimum benefit, proposed by the Carter Administration and substantially accepted in other bills put forward, could be a major factor in eliminating influxes of this sort.

The welfare debate and the consensus reached on many issues should be seen as a worthwhile attempt at the kind of comprehensive rethinking of policy that is required. On the important issues mentioned above and on a host of others, the consensus represents the foundation for a more enlightened approach in the future.

The present volume is more than a review of the debate arising from the introduction of the Program for Better Jobs and Income. It examines major issues in the welfare debate of 1978 in order to improve understanding of welfare reform and of the specific issues which are likely to be debated again in coming years. Only through such understanding will it be possible eventually to create a welfare system that is both just and efficient.

Leonard M. Greene
President
The Institute for Socioeconomic Studies

White Plains, N.Y.
July, 1978

ACKNOWLEDGMENTS

In the course of preparing this study, Samuel I. Eskenazi, of the staff of The Institute for Socioeconomic Studies, and I conducted interviews with officials of most of the governmental agencies, Congressional committees and interest groups cited here. All of the people we contacted were generous with their time and were most helpful in supplementing statements and positions advocated during hearings on welfare reform legislation. We greatly appreciate their help.

Special thanks are also owed to Bette K. Fishbein, staff economist of The Institute for Socioeconomic Studies, for the whole range of her aid, including help in assembling the comparison of welfare reform proposals, which begins on page 106. I am also obligated to two other Institute staff members, Frances T. Harte, editorial assistant and Roger J. Carlson, research adjutant, for the index. Lloyd R. Targer, another staff aide, worked on the Directory, which begins on page 113.

I also wish to acknowledge the invaluable assistance of Joan D. Viles.

Gordon L. Weil
The Institute for Socioeconomic Studies

White Plains, N.Y.
July, 1978

INTRODUCTION

The evolution of the nation's public assistance programs is measured by legislative milestones. In 1978, responding to the national protest over what the public increasingly holds to be the excesses and futility of "welfare" and spurred by President Carter's pledge to win enactment of a reform program, the Congress moved toward a consensus on proposals that would constitute a new milestone in development of a national policy on public assistance. During the course of the debate, some policymakers and spokesmen for groups advocating varying and conflicting reforms reached a new consensus on many welfare issues. As a result, they probably established a foundation on which debate in the 1980s will be based. For these reasons, 1978 is likely to be regarded as a generative point in the evolution of welfare policy. This is a report on the welfare debate of 1978.

Today's welfare program is the product of an evolution in public policy which began under the Administration of President Franklin D. Roosevelt. During his first term, a model of American society was developed which continues, in large measure, to be generally accepted. According to Roosevelt's experts, the economy should be made to function in such a way that anyone capable of work should be able to find a job at a level of pay sufficient to provide adequately for the worker and his or her dependents. The role of government would be to stimulate private sector employment, to set a minimum wage and to finance public works and public employment. Financial assistance would be provided to those who remained outside of the labor force for socially acceptable reasons, to those faced with temporary emergencies and to those who are involuntarily unemployed.

1

It should be obvious that the theory has never been fully applied in practice, especially as it relates to employment. In the years immediately following its development, the United States was plunged into a war which brought unparalleled economic growth and virtually full employment. In the next decade, attention was paid primarily to stimulating economic growth in the belief that the poor would benefit more from a stronger economy than from redistribution of wealth or income. Only in the 1960s did government begin to play a full-scale role in promoting the Roosevelt policy, and that effort has continued to the present.

During the Kennedy and Johnson Administrations, social policy, going far beyond such Rooseveltian programs as Social Security and the minimum wage, took the form of a series of new laws. The Area Redevelopment Act and the Manpower Development and Training Act were passed under Kennedy. Johnson's War on Poverty led to the passage of the Economic Opportunity Act. Other laws provided educational aid to disadvantaged children and welfare benefits to unemployed fathers. In addition, the social security system was expanded to provide social services and medical care. Moreover, through food stamps and commodity distribution, the Federal government began massive undertakings to help feed the poor.

At the same time, work went forward in the Johnson Administration on a comprehensive program of public assistance. It was based on the concept that government should provide public employment, the impetus for community social action and some kind of income floor in the form of a negative income tax. As Administration thinking evolved, planners came to the view that there should be an income floor, but that everybody should be able to climb from that floor only by his or her own work effort. In 1967, Congress adopted the Work Incentive Program (WIN), designed to provide financial work incentives to the poor and to require the employable poor to be referred to training and jobs. Because of the political obstacles to creation of a minimum income allowance, Johnson set up a Presidential commission to make a further study. In 1969, during the first year of the Nixon Administration, the commission reported itself in favor of a universal negative income tax. By that time, the new President had come up with his own version of welfare reform, involving a more limited negative income tax.

The Nixon Family Assistance Plan (FAP) emerged from a debate within the Administration. The starting point was a proposal by Richard Nathan of the Brookings Institution, patterned on the work already done by Johnson's experts. The Nathan plan did not survive because it did nothing for those poor or near-poor who did not qualify for specific categorical programs. Starting with a proposal generated by the Department of Health, Education and Welfare (HEW), Presidential advisor Daniel Patrick Moynihan fashioned what would ultimately become the FAP, a program which included aid for the working poor. Arthur F. Burns, one of President Nixon's most influential advisors, vigorously opposed such assistance. Eventually, however, it became part of the Nixon package.

Also, in 1969, President Nixon proposed expansion of the food stamp program. The issue had been precipitated by the introduction of legislation by Democratic Senator George McGovern to extend the existing, relatively small-scale food stamp program. Nixon's food stamp proposal, which was adopted, and the FAP, had it been adopted, would have amounted to a guaranteed income plan for all Americans.

The FAP died in Congress. Although the House twice passed versions of the Nixon proposal, a winning coalition could not be fashioned in the Senate. Alternative initiatives came from Senators Russell B. Long and Abraham A. Ribicoff. Long, the Democratic chairman of the Finance Committee, put forward his own plan, requiring work of most welfare recipients except for indigent mothers with pre-school children. Senator Ribicoff, a Democrat who once served as HEW Secretary in the Kennedy Cabinet, tried to salvage the FAP by proposing a more liberal version, designed to attract the support of liberals to the Nixon plan. Although the White House might well have been able to save the negative income tax if it had swung just ten votes, Nixon had apparently lost interest. The first major effort for a sweeping reform came to an end.

Still, all progress toward welfare reform was not halted. In 1972, Congress created, without significant opposition, Supplemental Security Income (SSI), a Federal program which replaced earlier state-run programs for the aged, blind and disabled. It was structured as a negative income tax. By 1974, the food stamp program had been expanded. As a consequence, it served to eliminate some of the inequities that are an inevitable part of categorical assistance. Such observers as Richard Nathan believe that these measures have gone a long way toward the creation of the kind of system that Nixon had originally envisaged when he introduced the FAP.

During the 1970s, political leaders had proposed a variety of programs to reform welfare. In 1972, HEW Secretary Elliot L. Richardson had his staff prepare a new proposal drawing on both the FAP and Senator Long's proposal. The plan was never introduced. During the Presidential campaign that same year, Senator McGovern proposed a flat, taxable payment to all persons, called a "demogrant." It was dropped after coming under heavy attack by Senator Hubert H. Humphrey. Later, the Joint Economic Committee's Subcommittee on Fiscal Policy, chaired by Representative Martha W. Griffiths, examined welfare policy. After a three-year study, it recommended a new version of the negative income tax. Although such legislation was introduced in 1976, it made no progress through Congress. In 1974, the new HEW Secretary Caspar W. Weinberger had his staff prepare a reform plan providing for a negative income tax that would replace and "cash-out" the existing welfare program, food stamps and SSI. President Ford refused to support it. In addition to all of this activity in Washington, state and local political leaders and many private groups came up with their own proposals for welfare reform.

By the time President Carter assumed office, the programs for aid to the poor had grown to encompass three major elements: social insurance, income support and jobs.

1) Social insurance programs provide assistance to people who have contributed to their financing and who meet certain eligibility criteria. Benefits are not related to need, so that people at all income levels may receive payments. The largest of these programs is Social Security (officially Old Age, Survivors and Disability Insurance or OASDI). In fiscal year 1976, it provided assistance to about 27.8 million American families. Although Social Security was originally planned as a work-related insurance program, it has been adjusted to reflect need as well as prior earnings. Unlike insurance, where benefits are often related to the amount of premiums paid, Social

4

Security provides proportionately greater benefits to low-wage workers than to high-wage workers.

Unemployment insurance is financed by payroll taxes on employees, although both the Federal and state governments may provide supplements under certain circumstances, particularly during periods of recession or persistent high unemployment.

Medicare has become another major social insurance program. It provides hospital health insurance to qualifying persons, age 65 or older. It is financed by premiums and by a payroll tax on both employers and workers. There is also a supplementary medical insurance program, paying part of non-hospital expenses, supported by premiums. In fiscal year 1976, some 24.5 million people were covered by Medicare.

The government operates a number of other social insurance programs including those covering retirement, workmen's compensation, and black lung benefits.

2) The income support system, representing only one-third of the cost of programs aiding the poor in their entirety, is need-related. Typically, recipients do not have to contribute to the system's support.

The most important of the income support programs is Aid to Families with Dependent Children (AFDC). Usually it provides cash aid to female-headed families with dependent children or those in which the father is unable to work. It is supported out of the general revenues of the Federal and state governments and, in some cases, localities. AFDC recipients may also receive benefits from other welfare programs. In fiscal year 1976, some 4.3 million families participated.

SSI pays cash assistance to the aged, blind and disabled on the basis of need. While the Federal government pays basic benefits, states may make supplementary payments. In fiscal year 1976, there were 4.4 million persons participating.

Food stamps, entirely financed by the Federal government, are provided to those in need and may be used in place of cash to make food purchases. Previously, recipients were required to pay a reduced amount for their monthly allotment, but the purchase requirement has been lifted and recipients are now given stamps in accordance with their need. Stamps are provided to those receiving AFDC and SSI, but other low-income people are also eligible for some food aid. In fiscal year 1976, some 7.7 million households received this kind of assistance.

There are also child nutrition programs which amount to an indirect subsidy for both poor and non-poor children. Among the programs are the school lunch and school breakfast programs. They are financed by state and Federal governments.

Medicaid provides medical care financing for the poor. Like AFDC, it is financed by Federal, state and, sometimes, local governments. In 1976, Medicaid paid for medical care for 23 million persons.

There are a great number of other major benefits programs, including housing assistance, basic educational opportunity grants, social service grants and veterans' pensions. In fact, The Institute for Socioeconomic Studies, working with Pace University researchers, found that 182 Federal benefit programs relating to income maintenance existed in 1977. They cost $248.1 billion, 69 percent of Federal tax receipts for the year.

Many states also provide emergency assistance to low-income people who encounter financial difficulties in any given month. Moreover, some states also provide general assistance for the needy who are ineligible for Federal cash assistance programs.

Finally, the earned income tax credit provides assistance to low-income wage earners by reducing their taxes at low-income levels. If a family's taxes are less than the value of the credit, any balance is refunded in cash.

3) Jobs are principally covered by the Comprehensive Employment and Training Act (CETA). Although CETA provides public service jobs for the cyclically unemployed, Title VI and, to a certain extent, Title II are specifically designed to help the poor and chronically unemployed. It is expected that programs for them will be increased under CETA in the future. At present, CETA provides financing, administered mostly by communities,

for 725,000 jobs. The WIN program, mentioned earlier, also provides some assistance to those on AFDC by offering training, job placement and incentives to private employers to hire the jobless. The WIN program is funded to the level of 200,000 positions.

Obviously, millions of people have come to depend on government for a part or for all of their income. Yet, there is an overwhelming consensus that there is much that is wrong with existing income maintenance programs, especially those designed for the poor. Government benefits reduce the number of people who would otherwise be classified as poor by as many as 33 million, but 12 million poor people remain, by the most conservative estimate. The poverty population may, in fact, be more like 18 million, even after almost all government programs are taken into account.

One of the reasons for persisting poverty is uneven coverage. While all poor people are eligible for food stamps, almost half are not eligible for other assistance. Yet, the estimated 46 percent of the poor who cannot obtain AFDC or SSI benefits have needs similar to those who can. Other kinds of gaps in coverage exist as well.

Even when people can obtain benefits, the amounts paid may be inadequate to allow them to rise above degrading standards. And, because of wide differences among benefits in various states, the greater Federal support for people living in one state as compared with another is considered by many to be unfair.

One of the most serious problems with many welfare programs is that their attempt to encourage work through requirements or financial incentives often brings about their own failure. Benefit reductions take place as earned income rises. When the benefit reduction rates of several supposedly complementary welfare programs are taken together, the result may well be a prohibitively high "tax" on earned income. In addition, there are vast administrative difficulties in enforcing work requirements.

Administrative weakness also appears in handling cash welfare benefits, with fraud and error rates higher than an acceptable level. To some extent, this weakness is the inevitable result of voluminous required paperwork.

Many welfare programs involve some degree of state financial participation. The burden, estimated at $15 billion in fiscal year 1976, is not well distributed, but falls most heavily on states with the largest welfare rolls. These states may face other severe financial problems and are reluctant to become involved in any welfare programs which tend to increase their own spending in the area.

Finally, the welfare system is highly decentralized and is not well integrated. There is no central control and no way to make welfare responsive to changes in national policy.

As a result of these problems with the current welfare system, sweeping changes appear to be needed. Undoubtedly, that was the reason so much attention was paid to the proposals for a negative income tax or similar mechanism. But, it should be noted, none of the negative income tax proposals has been adopted, in large measure because the inauguration of a reform designed to meet all of the major problems with the current system could carry a higher price tag, at least initially. The first element of the debate about welfare reform thus focuses inevitably on the shape of the program for solving problems which themselves are almost beyond debate.

COMPREHENSIVE VS. INCREMENTAL REFORM?

The current welfare system is a patchwork of programs that have been enacted over the decades. Each represents the consensus on welfare policy at the time of enactment and often embodies the response to a specific problem. Virtually nobody claims that the result is ideal. Many claim that, because "politics is the art of the possible," the current system is an accurate reflection of what was deemed by the President and Congress to be the best possible.

Some proponents of change suggest that today's political consensus, founded on a general dislike of the current system, would permit or perhaps even require a comprehensive reform in which many programs would be reshaped and some would be merged. They argue that, if there were no comprehensive reform, public dissatisfaction with welfare would continue to grow. Others continue to support the step-by-step or incremental approach in the belief that voters are not prepared to accept the higher initial costs of comprehensive reform and the uncertainty about how a new program would operate. Because President Carter's Program for Better Jobs and Income (PBJI) was based on the hypothesis that the time has come for a comprehensive reform, the debate on how to proceed has again been joined.

Basically, incremental reform seeks to improve the present system without changing its form. In the present context, it would mean that the categorical system of benefits would be maintained and administrative responsibility would still be divided among the Federal, state and local governments. It is possible that, if incremental reform is pursued persistently, the final result would be a system not significantly different from the one proposed by advocates of comprehensive reform.

9

Comprehensive reform might take any one of a number of paths, and there are wide divergencies among those who want sweeping change. Some suggest what amounts to a package of incremental reforms designed so that the programs could be shaped to meet common objectives. Others argue that many current programs should be replaced by a cash-payment system with greatly simplified eligibility requirements. Still others want to replace categorical aid programs with two systems, one for those expected to work and one for those not expected to work.

As the Carter Administration prepared its own welfare reform proposals, the strengths and weaknesses of all of these approaches were considered. Incremental reform was said to be the most attractive in terms of cost. In addition, it would be less likely to encounter resistance from both bureaucrats and members of Congress with vested interests in current programs. And there would be less uncertainty about how the reforms would actually operate as opposed to the considerable doubt about the actual application of the theoretical concepts of comprehensive reform. But a study by the Congressional Budget Office pointed out that "the basic disadvantage of the incremental approach is that, by building on the current system, it retains the basic weaknesses of that system: namely that it is a composite of ill-coordinated programs, each designed to meet individual objectives."

Among the possible approaches to comprehensive reform, the grouping of a number of incremental measures for simultaneous action is, of course, most akin to the incremental approach itself. But because each element in the package must be dealt with separately, there is no guarantee that the result will have the necessary degree of coordination or rationalization.

The discussion of a comprehensive cash program is complex and has gone on for a number of years. Perhaps it is best known to the public in the form of the negative income tax, given great currency by economist Milton Friedman in 1962. What seems most attractive about this approach is its administrative simplicity. However, political objections have been raised about the cost of the program and the possibility that people with incomes well above the poverty line would receive benefits. (This results from the use of benefit reduction rates set

10

in such a way as to encourage people to work. This issue will be discussed later.)

The work-welfare approach or track system is designed to avoid some of the high costs and benefits for those who are working. As a result, those who are not expected to work, such as mothers with young children, can be assured of reasonable public support payments without those benefits affecting the assistance and reduction rates applied to those who are expected to work. But a bureaucracy remains necessary to make determinations about which people are eligible for which benefits. In addition, a work-related system apparently would require both a training and placement program to equip the poor to take jobs in the private sector and a back-up program of government-provided jobs (public service employment) to provide work for those who cannot be accommodated by private business.

In the early stages of Administration consideration of the Carter welfare reform proposal, HEW Secretary Joseph A. Califano, Jr. seemed to lean toward the incremental approach. He had discovered that millions of Americans have come to depend on existing programs and would face the possible disruption of their lives if the benefits system was subjected to extensive and untested changes. In addition, he was aware that leaders of Congress had their own ideas about welfare reform and that most favored an incremental approach, improving programs which they had helped design.

But President Carter, believing that the present system shows all the defects of piecemeal design, instructed Califano and others to come up with a comprehensive approach. Virtually the only constraint Carter placed upon their deliberations was that the added cost be kept to a minimum. In fact, he believed at the outset that it would be possible to reshape welfare at *no* additional cost over current programs.

Three basic lines of thinking were reported to have emerged during the consideration of comprehensive reform. One would have had the government create public service jobs for all poor people who need work. Another would have been a form of the negative income tax. The third was essentially the track system. Ultimately, and in large measure because Carter himself did not have a specific plan in mind from the outset, the result was compromise among advocates of all three approaches within his Administration and between what might have seemed most desirable and what seemed to have the best chance of being enacted by Congress.

Carter's PBJI was billed as comprehensive welfare reform because it represented a break with present categorical programs, proposed to cash out AFDC, SSI and food stamps, would be linked with a jobs program, and would include a national minimum benefit. Yet, in one light at least, PBJI could be seen to have fallen far short of a genuinely comprehensive proposal. Of the 182 income-maintenance programs uncovered by The Institute for Socioeconomic Studies, PBJI would only consolidate three. Indeed, even if welfare were more narrowly defined, the PBJI did not deal with such major programs as housing subsidies and Medicaid.

"Several aspects of the proposal raise doubts as to its simplicity," said the American Public Welfare Association. The track system inherent in the PBJI led the APWA to conclude that "despite the unified program, many of the distinctions made by current programs among different categories of individuals and families will be retained ... Workers will still have to deal with a great many factors which vary from case to case. And, it is unlikely recipients will comprehend the program's many complexities." The APWA, assuming that a comprehensive reform should result in a less complex system in which savings could be realized from administrative streamlining, raised a series of questions about the obviously complex Carter proposal. "Consolidation of SSI, food stamps, and AFDC should result, at least over time, in the need for fewer persons to administer the unified program than were required to run the other three programs," the group admitted. "However, the fallout from this program may not result in less administrative effort in every state." In short, the APWA believed that simplification, an essential element of comprehensive reform, was lacking in the Carter proposal.

The introduction of the Carter proposal quickly elicited the opposition of Richard P. Nathan, once again a fellow of the Brookings Institution after service in the Nixon Administration. Nathan assumed the role of a leading opponent of the Carter plan, apparently not so much because he took issue with its substance, but because of what he considered its faulty, comprehensive approach.

Nathan suggested that much had happened since 1969, when the Nixon Family Assistance Plan was unveiled, to reduce the need for comprehensive reform. There have been massive increases in spending; the food stamp program provides aid to the working poor; a Federal program for the aged, blind and disabled has been created; work requirements have been enacted; and there are job programs for the poor. At the same time, public and political discontent with welfare has risen. "Why should we raise the issue of a new welfare program to high emotional pitch?" Nathan asked, worrying openly that the debate on comprehensive reform might finally conclude with the slashing of present programs.

Aside from consideration of need and political palatability Nathan said that the comprehensive approach embodied in the Carter plan "raised fundamental questions of cost, concept, and workability." By contrast, he argued that "multiple incremental reforms permit more flexible and realistic solutions than are possible by forcing all welfare cases into a single system."

Henry J. Aaron, himself a Brookings Institution alumnus and now Assistant Secretary of HEW for Planning in the Carter Administration, countered that while "it is possible, in principle, to identify one-by-one the shortcomings of the present programs . . . it is not possible to cure them one-by-one." He maintained that the incremental approach made administrative simplification and fraud reduction impossible. He also suggested that accomplishing the goals of welfare reform through incrementalism would carry a high price tag.

Another response to the Nathan criticism of comprehensive reform came from John L. Palmer, former HEW Director of Income Security Policy and now also at Brookings. He compared the welfare system to his aging auto. "Although continued repairs would have kept it running, and perhaps even improved it, it became clear that I could obtain a high level of performance only by trading it in for a new model."

Palmer argued that comprehensive reform must provide that "everyone has access to sufficient income assistance to attain a minimally adequate level of income," that "the overall welfare system ... be made simpler and more objective," and that "the work issue ... be dealt with constructively." He suggested that these objectives could not be achieved merely by repairing the current system.

But, as Nathan had indicated, the most powerful forces militating against comprehensive reform were political. Almost inevitably, comprehensive reform would mean adoption of a lower benefit reduction rate and higher breakeven point (where benefits are phased out) so as to provide both a work incentive to those on welfare and some income support to the working poor. But the fiscal implication of such a reform is bound to be higher overall costs, at least at the outset of the program. Raising Federal spending in this intrinsically unpopular area was bound to run into serious political opposition. That was why Nathan made specific proposals for incremental reforms, designed to move toward the objectives Palmer had outlined, but more modest than Carter's.

The kind of political difficulties that Nathan had foreseen were not long in coming. Leaders in both the House and Senate supported incremental alternatives to the PBJI on the grounds that they would cost less and thus be more likely of passage and of public acceptance. The unvoiced premise of their proposals was that members of the Congress would find it hard to justify increased welfare spending when they faced the electorate.

Representative Al Ullman, chairman of the House Ways and Means Committee, said as he introduced his own welfare reform plan that the nation "can't go on trying to buy reform." His appraisal of the political situation was forthright: "I don't think there is the time or the climate in Congress to push through a massive all-or-nothing welfare program this year." Although employing some of the rhetoric of the Carter proposal, Ullman was careful to draw the line: "My proposal is com-prehensive, but can be put into effect one piece at a time. It repairs existing programs in a sensible, economic way — rather than tearing down the entire system and rebuilding it at enormous cost and disruption."

In supporting the alternative introduced by Senators Howard H. Baker, Jr., and Henry L. Bellmon, Senator Abraham A. Ribicoff also followed the approach that the best might well turn out to be the enemy of the good. "This bill represents a moderate increment approach," he said. "As long as the choices in welfare reform are all or nothing, we will get nothing."

Senator Baker made it clear that one advantage of incremental reform was the possibility of proceeding without everybody involved being in agreement on the final form of the system. "Though some of the co-sponsors of this measure may differ as to what constitutes the ideal welfare system, we all share the view that welfare reform is essential and that it should be enacted this year," he said. The obvious implication was that Congress was not ready to undertake the kind of searching reexamination of the underlying premises of the welfare system that President Carter had sought.

Another powerful voice in opposition to Carter's comprehensive approach is Senator Russell B. Long, chairman of the Senate Finance Committee. Long has his own version of welfare reform in mind, involving a tough work requirement as a condition for receiving public assistance. In a gesture toward Carter, Long indicated that he might compromise with the Aaron view that it is impossible to implement pieces of the PBJI in isolation from the whole. Long has said that he is willing to support tests, limited in time and geographical scope, of the Carter proposal provided his own approach is also given similar treatment. The Baker-Bellmon bill also embodied the notion of experimenting, both with elements of the PBJI and with the approach favored by conservatives of making block grants to states and then allowing them to design their own programs.

Outside the Federal government, equally wide divergences of opinion exist on the overall shape of welfare reform. Most outside groups act as advocates for relatively well-defined interests and, rather than having to cope with the difficulty of coming up with a political consensus, they urge Congress to give their positions special consideration.

The nation's governors have a vested interest in the welfare system, but see it from a different perspective than many in Washington. In 1977, they were surveyed by the National Governors Conference. Of 47 respondents, 28 said they favored a single, need-related program. Only five supported a "continuation of existing categorical need-related programs." Yet their majority position should not be interpreted as being favorable to a change so radical as to permit the introduction of a negative income tax. In fact, only nine governors said they wanted a "guaranteed income program." One supported children's allowances and three said they wanted some other program.

A number of groups favor a comprehensive approach, but they are critical of Carter for having made a proposal which falls short of their specifications. For example, the National Association of Social Workers (NASW) found the broad outlines of the Carter proposal acceptable, but said: "We cannot help but express strong reservations at the flawed provisions and compromised principles." A similar position was adopted by the National Council of State Public Welfare Administrators (NC-SPWA). The National Urban League testified that "it is unfortunate that 'Better Jobs and Income' is not accompanied by the essential components of a full employment program and national health insurance program."

Some spokesmen are not so critical, Irwin Garfinkle, head of the Institute for Research on Poverty at the University of Wisconsin at Madison, has said he supports the comprehensive approach, because it does not single out the poor. The American Public Welfare Association, despite raising specific problems with the Carter plan, supports it.

In contrast, many labor unions are wary. The AFL-CIO's Bert Seidman has said that he would support a comprehensive approach, but that "if there's not a good welfare bill, we would support the incremental approach." Like the parent AFL-CIO, the American Federation of State, County and Municipal Employees would like to see food stamps kept as a separate program, thus undercutting a part of the Carter plan. Both unions have voiced deep concern about the wage rates in the jobs portion of the PBJI. These objections, if not met, would push them toward support for an incremental improvement of CETA and AFDC.

Robert B. Carleson, a leading conservative expert on welfare, has charged that the welfare establishment has limited the debate to a choice between comprehensive and incremental approaches. He has suggested that at least two other variations are possible. What he calls "comprehensive II" would return control over welfare to the states by increasing their funding through block grants. His "incremental II" approach would give states more authority over benefit levels and work requirements. In either case, plans for a guaranteed annual income or improvements in the present system would be abandoned. He has argued that his plan is politically acceptable because of the past successful record of general revenue sharing and the lack of public confidence in the Federal government.

The debate over comprehensive and incremental welfare reform is far from theoretical. It revolves around the chances for Congressional action and public acceptance. Cost is perhaps the determining factor. As a consequence, in 1978 Congress was not able to coalesce sufficient support to pass President Carter's PBJI. However, as with the FAP of the Nixon years, it may be that many of the objectives of the PBJI will be achieved by a series of uncoordinated decisions made by Congress over a period of years.

SHOULD WELFARE REFORM INCLUDE
A JOBS PROGRAM?

If press accounts of the Administration's development of the PBJI are correct, President Carter clearly engaged in some "zero-base" thinking. Believing that he was not tied to any existing income support program, the President appears to have tried to come up with an "ideal" reform package. The chief problem with this approach is that he, himself, had no vision of an "ideal" welfare system and his top aides had sharply differing views.

The result of Administration discussions was a compromise between a full employment program, under which the Federal government would commit itself to insuring a job for every American, and a cash benefit program, which would focus solely on those who need help and who are unable to work.

While the decision to include a jobs component in the welfare reform proposals could and would arouse debate, political realities pressed Carter to develop the two-pronged approach. Job creation is far more popular politically than is increased welfare funding. The title of the Carter plan — Program for Better Jobs and Income — allowed the Administration to candy-coat, if not disguise, the added welfare spending that President reluctantly came to believe was an inevitable consequence of reform.

The problem with a job guarantee as it emerged during Administration discussions, is that it can be immensely costly. And, as a study done by the Institute for Research on Poverty for the Joint Economic Committee indicated, "the mass creation of public service jobs for low-wage, low-skill workers is . . . fraught with uncertainty and the possibility of an ineffective and unproductive program must not be neglected." Problems also arise from the potential disruption of the marketplace, resulting inflationary pressures, administrative complexities and the possibility of capricious decision-making in determining who should work and who need not.

In explaining the jobs component of the PBJI to Congressional committees, Labor Secretary Ray Marshall made it clear that it was only meant to help the poor on their way to other jobs. The Administration proposal called for the creation of 1.4 million public service positions of which some 300,000 would be part-time. "We estimate that about 2.5 million workers each year would be expected to pass through these 1.4 million slots. This means that over the course of several years the great majority of the estimated seven million poor and near-poor families with children might be assisted by this program on their way to financial independence." Over 40 percent of those participating would be expected to be people currently eligible for AFDC.

Because there would not be enough jobs to provide a guarantee, the jobs element contains rationing features through eligibility criteria. Only adults in families with children would be eligible for the public service jobs to be created and only one adult per family would be able to participate. The wage level would be kept low as a way of encouraging people to seek higher-paying jobs elsewhere. At the same time, the Administration tried to keep wages at a level that would permit an adequate standard of living. The level targeted for 1981, the first year of the program, was $3.72 an hour, or $7,700 a year. Because states which supplement Federal cash benefits would have to supplement the Federal wage, in 37 states the average would be $3.83 an hour.

A controversial element of the proposal called for a five-week job search period during which the potential participant would have to attempt to find a slot in the private sector. He or she would be required to take such a job if it paid the prevailing wage, set at or above the subsidized wage. At the end of 52 weeks of public employment, the participant would have to undertake another five-week job search period.

The jobs program would be part of CETA and would be administered by local prime sponsors. The welfare-related jobs effort would become Title IX of CETA, and some of its funding would come from gradual reductions in spending under Titles II and VI. The Administration believes these shifts would be possible as the general level of unemployment declined. But it became clear during the debate on welfare reform that, if unemployment could not be reduced sufficiently, the Administration might have to continue CETA spending under Titles II and VI.

Because of the government's relative inexperience in creating and managing a jobs program of the kind envisioned in the PBJI, some doubts have been expressed about its ability to find a sufficient number of positions for the poor. Of course, some of the 1.4 million slots would be used for on-the-job training in an effort to bring the skills of the poor up to marketable levels. But the Labor Department has been at pains to illustrate that there are at least 1.4 million actual jobs that need to be done in society. Among the sectors it has listed are building and repairing recreation facilities, home services for the elderly and ill, public safety, child care, school paraprofessionals, community clean-up and school facilities improvement. It stresses that these are all to be jobs not now being filled.

Although the Carter Administration's concept of joining a jobs program to welfare reform received a generally favorable response, specific provisions were sharply criticized in Congress, by business and labor and by welfare groups. The proposal received its first thorough Congressional examination by the special Subcommittee on Welfare Reform Legislation, drawn from the House Committees on Ways and Means, Education and Labor, and Agriculture, and chaired by James C. Corman, a California Democrat.

The Corman Subcommittee made several important changes in the Carter proposal, reflecting some of the objections made by organized labor. Perhaps the most important was the adoption of a somewhat more generous provision concerning wage levels. In addition to authorizing payment at the Federal or state minimum wage, as had the Carter bill, the Corman panel also permitted wage standards to be set so that any employer would have to provide equal wages for equal work. The unions had been concerned that regularly employed workers would be replaced by lower-paid participants in the jobs program; the amendment was designed to alleviate this fear.

The bill, as changed by the Corman Subcommittee, also stated explicitly the wage levels that Secretary Marshall had forecast for 1981 and provided for a cost-of-living escalator.

Although the Corman version maintained the idea of a five-week job search requirement, it did not impose a similar period after 52 weeks of work. Instead, it simply provided that no person could participate in the program for more than 18 consecutive months.

In an attempt to placate opponents of the Carter plan, the subcommittee limited eligibility in the jobs program to those eligible for cash assistance. The Administration had wanted to include the near poor, many of whom might not be eligible to receive cash aid.

The net result of most of the Corman changes was to go part of the way toward meeting organized labor's most serious objections to the Carter plan. However, it was clear that labor would still be unhappy about the proposed wage levels. The changes proposed by the Corman group also promised difficulties on another front: the altered bill would surely cost more than the original Carter proposal.

The relatively few changes that the Corman Subcommittee made to the bill submitted by President Carter did not indicate broad Congressional acceptance of the PBJI jobs component. Al Ullman, chairman of the House Ways and Means Committee and one of the most influential Congressional leaders on any welfare reform measure, put forward a markedly different approach.

The Ullman plan provided for a much smaller jobs program, on the order of 500,000 slots. The vehicle for these would be the Work Incentive Program (WIN), not CETA. Ullman reasoned that the Administration's five-week waiting period was insufficient and substituted a 16-week period. He argued that many people would be content to wait out the comparatively short five-week period, but would, under the pressure of waiting 16 weeks without government aid, go out and find jobs of their own. In addition, Chairman Ullman argued that incentives under the WIN program would result in more people finding employment in the private sector. Like Corman, Ullman was unwilling to offer a job to the parent in a one-parent family.

This alternative focused on WIN rather than CETA because Ullman believed that WIN was better able to deal with employment of those on welfare. Indeed, it had been designed for this purpose. The vast majority of CETA workers, on the other hand, did not come from the welfare rolls. Despite criticism that relatively few people had found jobs through the WIN program in the past, Ullman argued that, properly funded, a public service employment program would have a better chance of success under WIN than under CETA. In effect, he said that WIN had not been given the chance in the past to do what he was proposing.

The Ullman alternative proposed to spend about half of what the Administration had sought for the jobs program. But Ullman maintained that the CETA program would remain intact and that no funds would be taken from it to finance welfare-related jobs, as Carter had proposed. He contended that CETA had turned out to be a form of disguised revenue sharing, providing funding that the states themselves would have made available in its absence.

A key aspect of the Ullman proposal was the simplification of the existing income tax credit available to private-sector employers who hire participants in the WIN program.

In addition, states would be rewarded financially for funding private-sector jobs for the poor. Such an approach had an obvious political appeal. Echoing the Carter line, Ullman told the Corman Subcommittee: "The bottom line of my program is jobs — with heavy emphasis on putting people back to work in the private sector."

In the Senate, the alternative to the Carter-Corman approach took the form of a bill introduced by Senator Howard H. Baker, Jr., the minority leader, GOP Senators Henry L. Bellmon and John C. Danforth and Democratic Senator Abraham A. Ribicoff. Known as the Baker-Bellmon bill, this proposal also aimed at an attempt to stimulate private-sector employment for the poor.

In a unique feature, the Baker-Bellmon jobs program would provide employers of the long-term unemployed or welfare recipients either a $1 per hour job voucher or a $1 per hour tax credit, at their option. Those eligible for jobs would be people on AFDC and those out of work for 26 weeks, provided they had sought work for a 90-day period. Former CETA workers would be eligible after 30 days of seeking work. "Our goal is to put people to work," said Senator Ribicoff. "It is better and cheaper to do for $1 per hour in the private sector than for $3 per hour in a public service job."

The sponsors of the Baker-Bellmon alternative also argued that CETA must be better targeted to reach the long-term unemployed. Although the current Title VI is supposed to benefit such people, it has not met expectations. Accordingly, Baker-Bellmon earmarks funding under this Title for some 375,000 long-term unemployed. This funding would be in addition to any other CETA spending, which had not yet been determined for 1981, the first year of the new welfare-jobs program.

As a relatively minor part of the proposal, the Baker-Bellmon bill provides for some reforms in the WIN program and a $200 million annual increase in funding to $565 million. It seems clear that the sponsors question the efficacy of the WIN program as the prime vehicle for stimulating employment of the poor in the private sector. However, they offer new provisions for job training under WIN.

The various proposals that have been advanced in Congress reflect attempts to develop a workable program in an area where past government activity has been relatively slight and to satisfy public demand, or what political leaders believe to be public demand, that as many people as possible on welfare be required to take jobs and as far as possible, that these jobs should be in the private sector. The feasibility of the various plans remains to be tested, but there are some indications of public and leadership sentiment. In a Harris poll after the introduction of the Carter bill, 81 percent of the sample supported the 1.3 million-job proposal and only 13 percent opposed it. In late 1977, the National Governors Conference asked governors, in a confidential survey, which program they would prefer for employable welfare recipients. Twenty-three favored a cash income maintenance system with a work requirement, 13 wanted direct government employment and a like number supported a government subsidy for private and nonprofit employment. (One favored a cash grant with no work requirement.) Both of these surveys reveal trends in opinion somewhat counter to those detected by proponents of alternatives to the Carter-Corman approach.

Although they are not opposed to the concept of a jobs program linked to welfare reform, the labor unions have expressed serious reservations about the Carter proposal. They worry that such a plan could result in the displacement of current public employees by lower-wage, government-subsidized workers.

The AFL-CIO wants jobs to be paid at the prevailing wage or the minimum wage, whichever is higher, and also wants fringe benefits, lacking in the Carter proposals, to be available to all workers. Even the Corman version's provision for equal pay for equal work is not acceptable to the union, because of the wage ceiling of $9,600 placed on the bill. This ceiling, the AFL-CIO argued, might negate the effect of the more generous Corman requirement.

Both the AFL-CIO and the American Federation of State, County and Municipal Employees (AFSCME) stress the need for a job guarantee to public workers who might be adversely affected by a new Federal jobs program. AFSCME, in particular, is concerned that regular workers could be displaced. It notes that the number of new slots that would become available in some cities would equal the present number of public employees. The temptation for cities to substitute low-wage workers for their current employees would be strong. Although there has been recent government action to crack down on illegal substitution under CETA, that program has come to provide a significant share of the jobs in many cities.

Among other changes advocated by the unions are Federal aid to state and local governments for their job training and placement programs and making public service workers eligible for the earned income tax credit.

The objections raised by organized labor have led some leaders, such as AFSCME's Jerry Wurf, to suggest that the best approach would be to separate the jobs program from welfare reform. Wurf believes that the prevailing wage rule would be more likely to be supported in an independent jobs program than in one that was welfare-related.

The Administration has tried to placate labor by making some concessions. It has cracked down on substitution in the CETA program and has promised to keep that program in operation at a relatively high level in those cities where the unemployment rate does not decline to a significant degree. As for the problem of two people doing the same job for unequal pay, the Labor Department has pushed the notion of the journeyman, a person with some work experience, assisted by the apprentice, in this case the new worker taken from the welfare rolls. Yet it appears unwilling to go as far as the AFL-CIO and such a major independent as the United Auto Workers of America (UAW) would like in raising the wage level.

Aside from the efforts made to alter the Carter jobs program in the Corman Subcommittee, labor has received support from elsewhere in Congress. Senator Daniel Patrick Moynihan, a New York Democrat, the architect of the FAP and the chairman of the Senate Subcommittee dealing with welfare, has attacked the Administration for proposing jobs that do not take into account the generally low skills of welfare recipients. "A jobs program will be a cruel hoax if it holds out the promise of unrealistic work," he said. Implicit in his criticism is the often-heard complaint that government would be unable actually to create all of the contemplated 1.4 million jobs.

Because of the jobs component, the PBJI has been referred to the Committee on Human Resources as well as to the Finance Committee in the Senate. A staff member at the Human Resources Committee has said that the Carter proposal is "a most significant advance over the FAP. It defines a group that is supposed to work and provides them with work." But he was critical of the wage provisions in the Administration bill and would prefer to see equal pay for equal work. He suggested that it might be possible to create jobs in sectors where they do not currently exist or to define current public jobs more narrowly as ways of avoiding substitution. He also argued for greater funding flexibility so that jobs could be stimulated in sectors where they are most needed and where workers are likely to be available.

Outside government, there has been strong criticism of the Carter jobs proposal, even from those who hail the Administration for its attempt to link jobs with welfare.

25

Both the National Association of Counties (NACo) and National Association of Social Workers questioned the adequacy of the number of jobs that Carter proposed. The NASW charged that the PBJI "creates a secondary work force . . . embodies needless coercive measures . . . establishes restrictive categorical work requirements . . . [and] does not answer the needs of the structurally or cyclically unemployed." In addition, the NASW argued that past experience with job search programs found them to be largely unsuccessful. As a result, the NASW called for "a manpower services delivery system" to support the job search program. Because of its doubts about the Carter proposal, the NASW openly questioned the linking of jobs and welfare in what it saw as a kind of workfare.

The American Public Welfare Association shared such concerns about the number of jobs and creation of a class of people who could suffer exploitation because of their low wage levels. It preferred pay at the prevailing wage. In addition, the APWA forecast serious administrative complications in the jobs program. Although the organization admitted that the Corman amendment which limited the jobs program to those eligible for cash assistance would make it more popular in Congress, one of its officials worried that this change represented a significant retreat from the Carter plan's movement toward a job guarantee.

The National Urban League was even more forthright in its criticism. "The jobs program should not be a component of welfare reform, but rather part of a full employment program," it said. Like other groups, it charged that pay levels were inadequate and fringe benefits lacking, that the denial of the earned income tax credit to those in public service work would create a two-class society and that there is no "specific help" offered for moving people from public service to the private sector.

Many of the views expressed by welfare organizations boiled down to a criticism of the Carter Administration for backing away from a full-scale job guarantee, regardless of the cost. These groups did not appear to accept the view that, without some link to the welfare system, a jobs program involving a broad guarantee would not be passed. Irwin Garfinkle of the Institute for Research on Poverty, countered that the advantages of the Carter approach could best be seen by noting the disadvantages of a job guarantee: the program would be larger, more expensive, attractive to more people than the economy could provide jobs and would be unsuited to meeting short-term unemployment problems.

Conservative groups were unanimously unhappy with the Carter jobs program. They suggested that people taking public service jobs might tend to stay in them permanently. They appeared to prefer a program in which any able-bodied person on welfare would be required to take a job offered by government. Robert Carleson also argued in favor of paying no more than the minimum wage as a way of providing an incentive for work in the private sector.

Among other conservative arguments voiced by the American Conservative Union and the Heritage Foundation was the belief that even those in public service employment would continue to receive cash assistance until they reached a relatively high income level. The Foundation also objected that the jobs to be undertaken are not needed — as demonstrated by the fact that the private sector has not already undertaken them. It questioned whether the poor had the requisite skills for the jobs proposed by the Labor Department. A Foundation report noted that previous job training programs had produced workers whose skills were not matched to society's needs. Conservatives also expressed doubts about job search programs and questioned whether they would be possible to administer. Finally, they noted that the largely untested jobs program could have an incalculable impact on the economy.

But, in sum, it appeared that Carter had been wise in proposing a jobs component in his welfare reform package. Yet, if he were forced to accept a more incrementalist approach in order to gain Congressional support, it was possible that a jobs program aimed at the poor might be separated from welfare reform and might be incorporated into an expanded CETA.

Congress seems increasingly interested in insuring that CETA provide jobs for people on welfare. As a result, the next step may be a study of the possible impact of a jobs program with final action deferred beyond the time when welfare reform decisions are made. Yet many in Congress, probably a majority, now believe that a jobs program as a part of overall welfare reform is an idea whose time has come.

THE BENEFITS PROGRAM

The jobs program is the vital element in Carter's PBJI, because it would constitute a government commitment to provide jobs for employable people who might otherwise be on welfare.

But obviously the PBJI is also based on the belief that there will always be millions of people who will require cash benefits from the government because they are unable to work. It holds that there will also be a pool of employable people who cannot find jobs and would thus be eligible for cash benefits. In addition, cash, in generally declining amounts, would also be provided to the working poor. Welfare benefits for these people would taper off gradually as their earned income rises and the benefit reduction rate would serve as an incentive for them to work rather than remain on welfare.

Three major sets of issues are raised in connection with the benefits program:
— Who will be eligible for government assistance?
— What benefits will be paid?
— Can the welfare system provide an incentive to work based on the rate at which benefits are reduced when a person begins to receive employment income?

Although each of these issues can be examined independently, it is obvious that they are closely interwoven.

WHO SHOULD BE COVERED BY THE WELFARE SYSTEM?

The simple answer to the question of who should be covered — many would say it is the simplistic answer —

is all those who are poor and need help. According to a fiscal year 1978 estimate, the Congressional Budget Office says that 8.9 million familes (10.7 percent of all families) live in poverty even when government programs are taken into account.

HEW Secretary Joseph A. Califano, Jr. has refined his data in recent Congressional testimony. He reported that between 1967 and 1972, some 21 percent of all Americans were poor in at least one year, but less than three percent were poor in all six years. By his reckoning, then, more than six million Americans appear to be permanently on welfare. Over 38 million more may be classified as poor in any given year.

Three types of coverage plans are under discussion in the debate on welfare reform legislation:

1. **Categorical.** This is exemplified by the current program which provides specific benefits to specific categories of people.
2. **Two-track or multi-track.** The Carter proposal is an example; it eliminates most distinctions among major programs, but distinguishes between those recipients who are *Expected to Work* (ETW) and those who receive benefits but are *Not Expected to Work* (NETW).
3. **Consolidated cash assistance.** This would provide a uniform benefit structure to all through systems such as a negative income tax or demogrant.

While the projected effect of each of these approaches in terms of adequacy and efficiency might be debatable, the general distinction among the three concepts is widely accepted. It should be noted that those who favor an incremental approach to welfare reform are talking about improvements in the categorical system. Those who now argue in the halls of Congress for comprehensive reform seek uniform national standards for eligibility. At the present moment, there is no serious legislative consideration being given to a consolidated cash assistance approach. But the Carter Administration would probably not be averse to having the PBJI characterized as a move in that direction.

The Carter proposal establishes universal coverage for cash assistance. All persons below a certain income level would be eligible for aid. The level is set in accordance with the size and composition of each filing unit. The program has been called comprehensive because, for the first time, the Federal government would make cash payments to single people, childless couples and many families where both parents are present. Under the current system, such people can receive food stamps which would be cashed out under the Carter proposal.

Those who would be classified as Not Expected to Work, NETW, would be the blind, aged or disabled and single parents with children under seven years of age. Single parents with at least one child between seven and 13 would be expected to work part-time during school hours. All others who have sufficiently low incomes to qualify for benefits would be classified as Expected to Work, ETW. That means that single people and childless couples would be ETW, as would one adult in two-parent families, and single people with no children under seven. These requirements are based on work customs in American society as a whole. Different benefits would be paid to those classified ETW than to those NETW.

Because there is a finite limit to the number of jobs that would be created in the public sector or, presumably, would be available in the private sector, the Carter plan establishes priorities in eligibility for jobs created under PBJI.

The filing or so-called household unit is similar to the sub-nuclear family unit currently recognized under AFDC and SSI. The Administration was convinced that simply defining the members of a family living together as the filing unit might work a financial hardship on aged, blind and disabled family members and on children receiving informal foster care.

Another factor affecting eligibility is the accounting period used in determining a potential recipient's income. The Administration proposal contains a complex formula which amounts to establishing a six-month period for establishing that income was low enough to qualify a person for benefits. The last month of the six-month period would fall two months before the month in which benefits were sought.

Finally, the assets held by a potential recipient would be

considered. After exclusions now included in the SSI program, including a house, household goods and a car, eligibility would be denied when non-business assets rose above $5,000. In addition, such assets would be considered to produce income. For non-business assets $500 higher than the allowed exclusions, income would be calculated at 1.25 percent of the asset value each month.

"More people would gain in income than would lose under the President's proposal," says the Urban Institute. The gainers would include those families with a member working for low wages, those in states with low benefit levels and people who fall through the cracks in the present system. Those now receiving AFDC and SSI would be assured of the same level of benefits, although new applicants meeting the same standards might receive lower benefits.

Secretary Califano told Congressional committees that some 36 million people would be eligible for jobs and cash benefits under PBJI, four million fewer than at present. Of the newly ineligible, one million are now receiving AFDC benefits. Tighter rules on stepfather units, increased job opportunities, the longer accounting period and the elimination of the work expense deduction would all serve to remove them from the rolls. The remaining three million are all now eligible for food stamps, although only one third of them actually participate.

Califano stressed that 32 million people — two million more than under the present system — would actually receive benefits. The increase would result from greater participation by people who are now eligible to receive food stamps, but do not, and from a simplified application procedure.

The Urban Institute notes that a larger share of total assistance would go to the most needy families under the PBJI eligibility rules. For families below the poverty level, 30 percent would be unaffected, 27 percent would lose benefits and 43 percent would gain. Single parent families would gain far more than intact family units.

When the Carter bill was considered by the Corman Subcommittee, some changes in eligibility standards were made, although the basic, universal approach was retained.

Universality was assured by including special provisions for foster children and institutionalized adults. The accounting period was made one month instead of six, so that benefits would be more readily available to people with fluctuating incomes. The assets test now used under SSI would apply, so that after exclusions, an individual's assets could be no more than $1,500 and a larger filing unit could hold no more than $2,250. In general, these provisions would increase the number of people receiving benefits, thus reducing the number of potential losers. Of course, they also increase the cost of the reform.

The alternative proposed by House Ways and Means Chairman Al Ullman is aimed at improving the present categorical system rather than at moving toward a more universal approach. While eligibility rules would be simplified, the resulting system would look similar to the current one. Ullman would adopt the same nationally uniform income definitions, accounting periods, work and reporting requirements and asset rules as for food stamps. Families with an unemployed breadwinner and a monthly income below $450 would be eligible for aid in all states. A one-month accounting period would be used to determine eligibility for all AFDC recipients. Such simplification might result in more people applying for welfare benefits.

The Baker-Bellmon proposal reflects much the same philosophy as is evident in the Ullman alternative. It would result in a slight increase in the number of people eligible for AFDC, because of the creation of a national standard for families with an unemployed breadwinner. A national minimum benefit level would be established at 65 percent of the non-farm poverty level in 1985. Some families with higher incomes and currently low benefit levels would be removed from eligibility. In addition, the bill would allow states to set up as many as three different eligibility standards, within national limits, to take into account differing conditions in different areas. The Baker-Bellmon proposal calls for using the SSI assets test for AFDC.

Although Senate Finance Chairman Russell Long has not begun work on any of these proposals, he has made it clear that he does not want to increase what he calls welfare "dependency" by "creating a new set of cash benefits for an entirely new set of recipients." As an example, he has cited the Carter plan to cash out food stamps. Recipients could become dependent on this money, he argued. He has said that the Carter plan could result in mushrooming expenses and has made it clear that he does not want to see a move toward a universal system.

The proposal to shift from a categorical approach to a two-track system has been one of the most hotly debated welfare reform issues, because of the recognition that it is the heart of the cash assistance proposal.

Support for moving away from categorical programs comes from a wide variety of groups, indicating a growing consensus that welfare reform requires an abandonment of the old formulas for a more universal and automatic system.

One of the most significant reactions to the future shape of the welfare system came in the National Governors Conference questionnaire. Twenty-eight governors favored a single need-related welfare program, while only five supported continuation of the existing categorical program. Nine more wanted a guaranteed income program and four others supported other approaches. On the question of who should be eligible, 32 thought that intact unemployed families receiving unemployment compensation should be added, 18 would have covered childless couples and 12 would have added single persons. In short, the governors indicated considerable support for the Carter approach, although only a minority supported coverage for most groups not now receiving benefits. But, in his testimony before the Corman Subcommittee, New York Governor Hugh Carey put the National Governors Conference squarely behind "a unified program for all eligible people below minimum income levels."

The National Conference of State Legislatures took much the same position. "We firmly believe that comprehensive regional reform is not only desirable, but possible," said its spokesman, Connecticut State Representative Irving Stolberg. "A tinkering or incremental strategy may yield some slight marginal improvements, but only at a cost of continued erosion of public support." He went on to call the two-tier system "a legitimate distinction." The NCSL also supported the shift to a one-month accounting period.

The National Association of Counties also gave its full support to the PBJI's coverage.

Major labor unions also lined up behind the universal coverage proposal. Bert Seidman of the AFL-CIO's Social Security Department told the Corman Subcommittee: "The AFL-CIO supports the thrust of the proposal which broadens the scope of welfare reform to include most of the disadvantaged ... in contrast to previous plans which have classified certain categories of needy Americans as being unworthy of assistance or incapable of working." Melvin Glasser of the UAW said the Carter Administration is "on the right track." The American Federation of State, County and Municipal Employees, an AFL-CIO union, gave its implicit support.

It is probably no surprise that organizations concerned with welfare administration, groups usually sympathetic to the needs of the poor, also supported the shift contained in the Carter plan. Steven A. Minter, president of the American Public Welfare Association, placed universal eligibility, as defined in the Administration bill, high on his group's list of priorities. A similar view was expressed by representatives of the National Council of State Public Welfare Administrators, but they explicitly favored the current assets test over the one proposed by the Administration.

Some groups, while generally favorable to the Carter proposal, said, in effect, that he had gone far enough. The National Association of Social Workers insisted that, even after food stamps were cashed out, a residual food stamp program should remain. According to the Carter plan, SSI eligibles would be placed under Federal administration. For both reasons, the NASW thought that the universal approach could actually create added administrative complexity. The NASW also found that the distinction between ETW and NETW recipients "promotes a strong disincentive to employment." The organization maintained that the jobs program "should not separate people by categories or work expectations, nor penalize them for wanting to work." The NASW argued that jobs should be offered to all who want them, thus reducing welfare costs and shifting the resources to job creation. The National Urban League took a similar position against the ETW and NETW categories, urging that "there should be both vertical and horizontal equity" — that all people in the same financial condition should be treated in the same way.

The New York-based Center on Social Welfare Policy and Law took a close look at the ETW and NETW classifications and found what it claimed were loopholes. It suggested that the Administration failed to provide for people between the ages of 16 and 21 and that it was unclear how a two-parent family with one parent over 65 would be treated. The special treatment of single parent families with a child between seven and 13 came in for criticism, with the Center charging that their inclusion under a part-time work program was the result of a compromise between Administration views and those of Senator Long. The Center felt that this measure made it difficult for parents with young children to undertake work in the home, usually in childcare activities.

Outright opposition to the move away from categorical programs was inherent in the objections and alternatives of Senators Long, Baker and Bellmon and Representative Ullman, all of whom may have a decisive influence on the ultimate shape of welfare reform legislation. They feared escalating welfare costs and increased dependency of people on welfare benefits.

The American Conservative Union's Welfare Reform Task Force took the position that "welfare benefits should go only to those in need and benefits should be sufficient to meet basic needs only." To the ACU, that meant that able-bodied people should be required to take an available job or assist in their communities as a condition of getting any help. "For the able bodied," the ACU said, "for that period when no work is available, assistance should be in the form of food (or food stamps), clothing, housing and necessary medical and other services." Its thesis was that such benefits would be an encouragement for those temporarily in need to seek jobs; cash benefits for all those below a certain income would encourage them to accept welfare rather than seeking work.

Although ACU task force member Robert B. Carleson has served as a consultant to the United States Chamber of Commerce and despite the conclusions of at least one informed observer that business would not favor a proposal that moved toward income redistribution, the Chamber's Council on Trends and Perspectives has said that "the frequently-heard statement that welfare benefits should be confined to 'the truly needy' may have an appealing sound, but it does not provide an approach to welfare reform." Its report concludes: "It is the Council's firm belief that time and energy now being spent trying to improve or streamline existing programs would be far better spent designing a sound plan to replace these programs with cash transfers made through the income tax system."

To a great extent, the debate over the incremental versus the comprehensive road to welfare reform is centered on the orientation of policy toward recipients. Although the PBJI is a long way from income redistribution, it symbolizes the first major step away from the conservative view that help should only be given to those in need and then only through programs with large, non-cash components.

WHAT BENEFITS SHOULD BE PAID?

The Carter Administration's benefit proposals would set a Federal minimum income of $4,200 for a family of four (including only one adult). HEW Secretary Califano discussed the reasons for setting benefits at the levels proposed. "The decision to set benefit levels for a non-aged, blind or disabled family of four at $4,200 was not an easy one," he told the Senate Subcommittee on Public Assistance. "It is clear that it is economically impossible and undesirable to set Federal benefits at the level of the highest state. On the other hand, the benefit could not be set so low as to cause a hardship on present recipients." The $4,200 level was higher than current Federal spending on AFDC and food stamp benefits in all but seven states.

The "building blocks" of the program, according to Califano, were as follows:

Household unit member	Annual benefit
An adult, aged, blind or disabled (ABD)	$1,600
Any other adult	1,100
A child, blind or disabled	1,100
Any other child	600

If the unit consists of:	Bonus
One adult, ABD	$900
Individual and spouse, both ABD	550
One adult and one or more children	1,300
Two or more adults and one or more children	800

Thus, a family of four, consisting of a mother and three children, would receive: $1,100 + 600 + 600 + 600 + 1,300 = $4,200.

These building blocks apply to those Not Expected to Work (NETW). Lower benefits are available to those who are Expected to Work (ETW). The adult in the ETW category is dropped from the unit and $800 is thus subtracted from the bonus.

There are other deductions in the Carter plan. When two household units share space, their joint benefits are reduced by $800. No household can receive benefits for more than seven people.

The distinction between upper and lower tiers is vital to the Carter program.

	Upper Tier	Lower Tier
Individual (ABD)	$2,500	$ —
Couple (ABD)	3,750	—
Individual	1,100*	0
Two-parent family of four	4,200*	2,300
Single parent family of four	—	—
Youngest child under 14	4,200	—
Youngest child 14 plus	4,200	2,300

Those benefits marked with an asterisk are only paid to an ETW person when there is no employment available. After an eight-week job search period, a lower tier person can be moved up. If an ETW person refuses a job, however, that person can again be dropped to the lower tier. Given the operation of the benefit reduction rate, the upper and lower tiers gradually merge as earned income increases. Upper tier people who are not required to seek employment may do so without being dropped into the lower tier.

In addition to those Federal benefit standards, the Carter program would improve the earned income tax credit (EITC) available to low-income people working in the private sector. The EITC is discussed later with regard to the work incentive.

Upper tier benefits were set at levels designed to protect current entitlements to AFDC, SSI and food stamps. Lower tier benefits were designed to protect current entitlements to food stamps. However, there would be some who would lose benefits as a result of the new program.

State supplementation of Federal benefits would, just as at present, continue to be possible. Substantial Federal assistance toward that end would be available. Because the proposed Federal benefit would be about 65 percent of the poverty level, states choosing to hike the benefit level to 75 percent would be able to avail themselves of Federal help providing three-quarters of that ten percent increment. The Federal government would pay states one-quarter of the cost of bringing benefits up from 75 to 100 percent of the poverty level. In addition, the Carter plan would provide an incentive for states to maintain existing benefit levels by assuring them of promised fiscal relief of at least ten percent. The Administration anticipates that most states will choose to keep benefits at current levels. One caveat: only state supplements which honor Federal eligibility rules would be subsidized.

The Corman Subcommittee adopted the same cash assistance structure as in the PBJI, but approved a number of measures whose combined effect would be to increase total benefit amounts. It removed any limit on the size of the family that would receive aid, in contrast with the Carter plan's limit of aid to no more than seven in a family. It also provided for more generous Federal matching of state supplements. In some cases, the Subcommittee removed the $800 deduction from benefits when two household units occupy the same dwelling.

The Corman panel also put benefits on a permanent cost-of-living escalator. The Carter plan, in contrast, would require legislative action in order for benefits to keep pace with inflation.

Unlike the Carter plan, the Corman bill would not allow other income-related programs to count the cash-out value of food stamps as income; the result would be higher total benefits for people receiving assistance under other programs.

Finally, the Subcommittee would not completely abolish food stamps. Although as a general rule they would be cashed out, some would remain available to people whose total cash income was below the eligibility level in the food stamp program.

On the other side of the ledger, the Corman proposal provides for recoupment of excess benefits through income taxes.

In line with its incremental approach, the Ullman bill adopts some portions of what was proposed by both the Administration and the Corman Subcommittee. Perhaps most important. Ullman accepts the minimum benefit amount of $4,200 for a family of four. Because he does not favor cashing out food stamps, their cash value is included in this amount. The Ullman bill would mandate an AFDC-Unemployed Parent program so that intact, two-parent families would come under the program. Other groups not now receiving cash benefits would continue to be limited to food stamps. Indeed, the cash amount does not vary according to family size; food stamps are the variable element in the minimum benefits package. As noted elsewhere, the Ullman plan calls for a greater tax benefit under the EITC as a way of encouraging private sector employment.

The Ullman plan includes provisions for recoupment of excess benefits through the income tax system. When annual gross income, less child care expenses, exceeds the food stamp phase-out point by more than $2,000, some AFDC and food stamp benefits would be recovered by the government. (Proponents of the PBJI claim that a feature of the six-month accounting period would prevent the payment of excess benefits. If income exceeded allowable limits in any one month during the period, the excess would be counted as part of the following month's income. As a result, the amount of benefits for which a recipient might be eligible for the second month would be reduced.) As part of the effort to prevent excess payments, the Ullman plan also calls for taxing unemployment compensation benefits. His aides point to abuses in the present system and indicate that he regards unemployment compensation as a social welfare program, not a form of fringe benefit for workers.

The Baker-Bellmon bill would also establish a minimum benefit amount, set at 65 percent of the poverty line in 1985. Payments to lower-income families in the AFDC program should increase as a result of a proposed increase in the amount of earned income that would be disregarded before determining the recipient's cash benefits. In addition, the elimination of certain higher income families from AFDC would increase the average benefit of the less well-off, according to the Congressional Budget Office. Average benefits under the AFDC-Unemployed Parent program, which would be reformed and extended, could be expected to rise by seven percent. States would be expected to continue supplementing Federal benefits, but could expect the Federal government to assume, by fiscal year 1982, as much as 80-90 percent of the cost of benefits which (when combined with food stamps) equal the poverty line. In short, the Baker-Bellmon bill calls for a moderately incremental program, in terms of cash benefits.

To judge from a 1977 Harris poll, there appears to be broad public support for the Carter approach. The benefit levels in his plan are approved by 77 percent of the sample and disapproved by only 12 percent. The EITC received similar support.

However, a clear majority of the governors surveyed by the National Governors Conference have some trouble with the two-tier approach. Although they were aware that the rationale underlying this scheme is to encourage welfare recipients to seek work, 31 of the 39 responding governors did not approve of it and only five did.

Among the most unequivocal supporters of the Carter plan were the National Association of Counties and the National

Governors Conference. The National Conference of State Legislatures also went on record in favor of the proposal, although it argued that no person's benefits should be reduced and that new applicants who would have met former eligibility standards should receive benefits at the former level. Such changes would increase the cost of providing benefits.

An array of arguments were suggested by groups who felt that the Administration had not gone far enough. Senator Daniel Patrick Moynihan, chairman of the Senate Public Assistance Subcommittee, led those claiming the $4,200 benefit was too low. The AFL-CIO representative said that "the proposed levels are inadequate by even the poorest of standards. They fall far below the poverty level which is based on a bare austerity diet providing little else that the family needs to live on besides a rock-bottom minimum of food and shelter." The UAW argued that the minimum benefit should gradually be increased to the poverty level. Newark Archbishop Peter L. Gerety, speaking on behalf of the U.S. Catholic Conference, said that cash assistance benefits "do not meet minimal expectations for reform." Other groups which have said that the $4,200 is inadequate include the National Association of Social Workers, the Gray Panthers, the Center on Social Welfare Policy and Law, and the National Welfare Rights Organization.

State supplementation provisions have come in for criticism from much the same group of organizations. They recognize that what they regard as inadequate benefits are only likely to be raised by state payments. Yet the Carter plan provides incentives for continued supplementation; it does not require such state spending. The National Council of State Public Welfare Administrators said the 52 percent benefit reduction rate would actually discourage supplementation, because the cost would be so high. (Corman has met this objection.) These groups want supplementation made mandatory.

A number of other specific provisions have been sharply attacked. Against the background of opposition to the six-month accounting period, there was also criticism by the NASW and the AFL-CIO of even the one-month period. They argued that the system of prior month budgeting actually means that judgments will be made on the basis of a month which fell two months prior to the application for welfare. They support a determination of need made at the time of application. "It is unreasonable to think that a family that had earnings slightly above the poverty line two, three or six months earlier will have been able to save much money," said Senator Moynihan. Dorothy Lang, an attorney at the Western Center on Law and Poverty and a counsel in a case against California's prior month budgeting system, told of cases where families, deserted by the principal breadwinner, were unable to receive benefits until months later. People have been forced to accept meager diets and eviction, according to Lang, because they could not save any excess receipts for use when payments were later cut.

The NASW, the National Urban League, and the American Public Welfare Association were among the groups criticizing the reduction in benefits for people ETW, during the job search period. Said Steven Minter, president of the APWA, "The important thing to note is that this 'penalty' is imposed at a time when the primary wage earner is totally dependent on the private sector — and later the public sector — to provide a job and he/she can do little or nothing to impact on job availability." Of course, household expenses do not decrease during the job search period.

Several groups, including the U.S. Catholic Conference and the APWA, argued for automatic indexing of welfare benefits to ensure the welfare recipient against loss due to inflation.

Objections were also raised to the penalty levied when two receiving units occupy the same dwelling. The NASW claimed that the $800 benefit loss discourages intergenerational households and prevents sharing resources which reduces the number of households in poverty. In addition, the NASW claimed that the method of deducting the $800 discriminates against those with less resources. Speaking on behalf of the Gray Panthers, Maggie Kuhn said that "an elderly woman who moves in with her elderly sister for mutual care and companionship will find that her benefits are reduced by $66.00 a month!"

Perhaps the harshest criticisms were directed against the two tier benefits. Testifying on behalf of the NASW, New York welfare official Carol Parry said that the Carter plan "is inequitable in that differential payment levels are established for families with children, the non-aged and able-bodied, childless couples and the aged. Social services cannot be expected to substitute for inadequate income payments. At a minimum, all categories of individuals and households should receive the same percentage of assistance payment ..." Another NASW statement said that the distinction between ETW and NETW "promotes a strong disincentive to employment and does not recognize the individual's desire for work and/or training and particular skill level." The Urban League also argued against placing people in categories. Senator Moynihan argued that "the Administration's proposed penalty for refusing to accept work is severe. A family's benefit will be cut nearly in half (45 percent) if its head does not accept a job."

Opponents said the two-tier system would harm family structure and hit certain people especially hard. "The Administration's plan does not eliminate incentives for families to break up," said Senator Moynihan. In a two-parent family, only the primary wage earner is eligible for a public job. This runs counter to the current trend of increasing numbers of two-earner families.

Moreover, if a father secures a job in the private sector, he can "desert" his family. The wife thereby becomes eligible for a public job. This can significantly increase total family income. A single parent family of four has a basic grant of $4,200. A two-parent family of four has a basic grant of $2,300. If a father deserts and there are children under age seven, the family becomes eligible for the higher grant.

A deduction of up to $300 per month is permitted for single parent families. This deduction with a marginal tax rate of 50 percent is equivalent to $1,800 a year in cash. A father can make his family eligible by deserting.

The incentive for family break-up that opponents of the two-tier system find can be easily illustrated.

Example: two-parent family of four, children under age seven, father earning minimum wage.

If family stays intact:

Father's Income	$ 5,512
Cash supplement	1,444
Total income	$ 6,956

If family splits:

Father's income	$ 5,512
Cash supplement	3,600
Total income	$ 9,112

If family splits and mother takes public job:

Father's income	$ 5,512
Mother's income	5,512
Cash supplement (after child-care deduction)	3,244
Total income	$14,268

A study prepared for the JEC by Professors Robert Haveman and Eugene Smolensky of the University of Wisconsin reported results of a computer-based test of eliminating the two tiers. "The implications of this change are very modest," they noted, "while cash benefits rise by four percent, the cost of the jobs program falls by five percent, leaving a net increase in program costs of $0.4 billion." The authors admitted that "some judge that this change will make the task of getting people to seek jobs more difficult by reducing one of the penalties for not working." Yet, they concluded that "the increase in costs would be likely to yield some increased poverty reduction as well as simplify the proposal."

Voices seeking more and more generous welfare benefits are balanced by those with more moderate views, including Representative Ullman, and Senators Long, Baker and Bellmon. Richard Nathan, the advocate of incrementalism, sets forth a strong series of arguments for attempting to keep a rein on costs.

Nathan accepts a national minimum standard, but proposes that it be set at $4,000 for a family of four under AFDC, as opposed to Carter's $4,200. He also advocates a mandatory Unemployed Parent element of AFDC; he would agree to an all-cash payment instead of a food stamp element. However, food stamps would be used, as at present, to provide benefits to single people not covered by AFDC. This approach is the essence of incrementalism as compared with the Carter Administration's comprehensive formula. Because of some similarities, Nathan could tell the Corman Subcommittee that his approach "would enable us to move faster on items in the Carter welfare reform program that are widely agreed upon and can be relatively quickly enacted."

In reacting to the Carter proposal, the American Conservative Union argued against a national benefit standard. Its welfare reform task force believed that under the Carter proposal, benefits will go to people who should be disqualified because they earn some income. More importantly, ACU says that "the welfare problem and its solution may be different for each recipient or each family ... The essence of an efficient and effective system of income redistribution is the elimination of complexity and the introduction of uniformity. On the other hand, the essence of a true welfare system is a system geared to meet the basic needs of those who through no fault of their own are in need of public assistance." For the ACU, the Carter PBJI is a form of income redistribution.

Seen in the context of the debate, the Carter benefit levels appear to be the highest that can be achieved. Even if an incremental approach is adopted, it is likely that the benefit level will be somewhat higher than Nathan had proposed.

CAN THE WELFARE SYSTEM ENCOURAGE PEOPLE TO WORK?

Many critics of the current welfare system say that it offers benefits that make it more attractive for the recipient to stay home than to go to work. As a result of such beliefs, increasing attention has been paid over the years to the interrelationship between welfare and work.

Even so, that interrelationship is sometimes still challenged. Former HEW Secretary Elliot L. Richardson has, for instance, contended that, of all those receiving AFDC who do not work, only 18 percent are fit for employment. In other words, no jobs program could move the vast majority of welfare recipients off of public assistance. But many Congressional leaders would argue that Richardson's definition of "not fit for employment" is unduly permissive. Clearly, in World War II as

45

well as other instances, great numbers of "unemployables" were brought into the economy and assumed highly productive responsibilities.

In an effort to reduce dependence on welfare, Congress has over the past 16 years enacted a number of jobs programs intended to provide work for people who might otherwise be on welfare. However, a study by Ned L. Young of the *Baltimore News American* concluded: "an examination of past manpower programs does not prompt too much optimism for the future." Young found that virtually all Federal jobs programs had been ineffective in reducing unemployment, particularly among the poor.

Young suggested that among the reasons for failure were defects in program design of plans at CETA and WIN. But, most importantly, he found that government programs fail to provide an adequate financial incentive for people to take jobs. Milton Friedman, the Nobel laureate in economics, criticizes similar instances of government myopia. According to Dr. Friedman, by continually increasing the federally mandated minimum wage, Congress actually makes it more difficult for disadvantaged young people to enter the work force. Employers are reluctant to pay such unskilled labor at the required rate.

In the debate over welfare reform, the rate at which benefits are reduced as earned income increases has become a major issue. This benefit reduction rate is coming to be understood as having a preeminent impact on the willingness of people on welfare to take available jobs. Further, some argue that it is possible to adjust the so-called benefit reduction rate in such a way as either to encourage greater employment in the private sector or to stimulate it in the public sector.

HEW Secretary Joseph Califano made the basic case for work incentives through the benefit reduction rate when he testified before the Corman Subcommittee on Welfare Reform:

> The system of "benefit reduction rates" is designed to address a fundamental problem: if cash benefits are reduced at too steep a rate as earnings increase there will be no incentive for work.

For example, if the cash benefit is reduced by $1 for every $1 earned, there is obviously no work incentive whatsoever.

If the cash grant is reduced 90 cents for every $1 earned, there still may be no incentive, because travel costs and other expenses of going to work will mean there is still little or no real improvement in the individual's financial condition as the result of employment.

But, there is also a problem at the other extreme. If the cash benefit is reduced by only 25 cents for every $1 earned, there is a good incentive to work (income increases by 75 cents, less work-related expenses for every $1 earned), but families will continue to receive cash assistance at income levels that seem much too high to many taxpayers.

In short, the benefit reduction rate must be low enough to encourage people to take jobs, but not so low as to push the point where all benefits are phased out to an income level where society believes that no public assistance should be paid.

Cut-off or breakeven points that exist in today's welfare "system" can have the effect of severely penalizing a poor person. As little as an extra dollar of earned income can strip away extensive benefits (e.g. food stamps, Medicaid, housing). The obvious consequence of the cut-off points and of sharp "benefit reduction rates" is to discourage the poor from seeking work.

The necessary consequences of the slow tapering off of benefits for the employed person is that some small amount of benefit dollars will be paid as the recipient's earned income rises to appreciable levels. Writing in *THE JOURNAL/The Institute for Socioeconomic Studies,* Senator Daniel Patrick Moynihan warns " ... we can find ourselves in situations where persons with absurdly high earnings can still receive welfare benefits." Dr. Blanche Bernstein, New York City Human Resources Administrator, has testified that under the present law it is possible in New York — though admittedly not likely — for a person to

47

have a total annual income reaching $29,000 before the last dollar of AFDC payments disappears. And as long as there is even a single dollar of AFDC being paid, that person and his or her family retain full eligibility for Medicaid.

In House testimony in opposition to the Carter PBJI, Representative Dave Stockman of Michigan made a strong case against high benefit reduction rates. He attacked welfare benefits that are often higher than net earned income for people in low-paying jobs. Family break-up, he pointed out can be encouraged.

By leaving his family — or appearing to do so — a father continues to collect his earnings, while the mother and children now become eligible for full benefits. As a further illustration of the way benefit reduction rates undermine parental responsibility, Stockman said that child-support payments from an absent father impose a reduction upon the mother's government benefits of almost 100 percent. Incentive for the father to pay is at least commensurately cut. The Michigan legislator also charged that the present system and the one proposed by Carter involve an excessively complex administrative apparatus to insure that welfare recipients are meeting complicated and cumbersome requirements.

Some, however, make an effort to dismiss the significance of work disincentives and of benefit reduction rates. New York Governor Hugh L. Carey testified that, "in the real world, the marginal economics of 'low benefit reduction rates' is not what makes people work. When decent jobs at decent wages are available, most welfare recipients, out of pride and self-respect, will take them eagerly."

Nevertheless, there is widespread awareness that the welfare system can effectively undermine the determination to work. The "notches" associated with benefit reduction rates are particularly destructive in this respect. Columnist Louis Rukeyser has reported on the pressures imposed upon the poor:

Let's focus on a typical deserving member of the working poor: a married man with two children, living in Los Angeles and earning $4,800. Since he is certifiably poor, he is eligible for substantial tax-free payments:

48

food stamps, low-income housing, welfare, unemployment insurance where applicable, and so on. But as his earned income rises, he comes up against an unpleasant fact that middle-income poverty workers seldom headline: He's better off remaining poor (and remaining dependent on the poverty workers' bureaucracy) ... the worker with annual gross earned wages of $4,800 would actually have each month in net spendable income (wages plus government benefits) $810.49. That, incidentally, would be only $92.94 more than the family would receive if he wasn't earning a penny.

But it gets worse. At the $4,800 level, every time he earns a new dollar, he loses so many benefits that his real income increases only 5.2 cents. That's an effective marginal tax rate of 94.8 percent. (The highest official tax code goes is 70 percent, and that's only for taxable incomes over $200,000.)

And if you think that's bad, consider what would happen if he did get that 50 percent raise — to $7,200 a year. His net monthly spendable income would be down from $810.49 to $784.76. And if by some miracle he doubled his earnings, to $9,600 a year, he'd really feel stupid — for his net family income would have fallen even further: to $773.82.

Indeed, at both these income levels, his effective marginal tax rate would be over 105 percent; every dollar he earned would put him further behind (even when he really surged ahead and started earning $12,000 a year, the monthly net — $795.94 — would be less than he had to spend with a theoretical $4,800 income).

Actually, it is even difficult to determine the effective marginal rates in the current system because the various income maintenance programs are complex and vary among states. In general, food stamp benefits are now reduced by 24 cents for each dollar earned, after $60 per month and child-care and shelter expenses of up to $75 per month are deducted from earnings. As for AFDC, the general Federal rule sets the marginal tax rate at 67 cents for each dollar earned after the first $720 earned in a year. This amount is called the "minimum disregard." However, many states allow additional disregard amounts based on child-care and work-related expenses. The Urban Institute estimates that the net impact of these disregards, in addition to the $720, amounted to 31 cents of each dollar earned. Combining the minimum and additional amounts, it says that there is an estimated total AFDC disregard of 64 percent of earnings. That calculation would mean that the effective marginal tax rate would be 36 cents out of each dollar earned. It is actually a good deal higher, because it must be combined with the food stamp rate and the rates implicit in other programs such as Medicaid and public housing to determine the overall rate.

The Carter proposal, which would cash out food stamps, would introduce new rates, adjusted depending on family structure. In general, benefits would be reduced by 50 cents for each dollar earned. For two-parent families and single parent families with children under 14, the rate would only apply to earnings over $317 per month. In those states which choose to supplement the Federal benefits program, the rate might be raised to 52 cents. The 50-cent recovery rate would apply to other single parent families with children, after a deduction for child-care expenses. Where states supplement Federal benefits, the recovery rate for these people might go as high as 70 cents.

Of course, once a person begins to earn wages, he or she is subject to income taxes. For that reason, there is an earned income tax credit (EITC), designed to prevent such a large recovery of money by the Federal government as to discourage work. At present, a ten-cent credit is provided for each dollar of income up to $4,000 per year. The credit is reduced by ten cents for each dollar earned above $4,000. In the Carter plan, there would be a ten-cent EITC for each dollar of income earned in the private sector up to $4,000 a year and five cents per dollar up to $9,100 for a family of four. Once a family has passed the income level which permits it to receive cash benefits, the credit would be further reduced until it is phased out. The breakeven point would be $15,650 for a family of four.

The Urban Institute has made comparison of the present

system with the Carter proposals and finds that they do not yield a consistent pattern. For single parent families with young children under the PBJI, rates are higher into the middle range of possible earnings. The probable impact of the benefit reduction rate would be to discourage affected people from seeking part-time work. However, there would be a stronger work incentive in the Carter plan for full-time employment, based on lower effective rates above $6,000.

The situation would be sharply different for two-parent families. Up to the level of $4,000 in earnings, the tax rate would be well below current levels. A "notch" serving as a strong disincentive to work would be eliminated by the PBJI for those employed for more than 100 hours per month. Above the $4,000 level, the current system and the Carter proposal have similar rates.

When the Corman Subcommittee considered the Carter bill, it took a series of actions which resulted in reducing the work incentive inherent in the Administration's tax rates. Among the changes were a provision to allow a tax rate of up to 70 percent in states providing supplementation for all welfare recipients, a phase-out of the EITC at $4,200 for a family of four instead of Carter's $9,100 and making assistance payments subject to the Federal income tax.

Within the Corman proposal, the major difference with both the current system and the Carter plan would be the high rates for two-parent families with earnings from $4,000 to $9,100. The Urban Institute has found that under the Corman approach, there would be "virtually no financial work incentives for part-time workers to seek full-time jobs, for low-wage workers to seek higher paying work or to take a second job, for the low-wage worker's spouse to look for work or for the public sector worker to show up on the job every day or to try to find a better-paying job in the private sector."

Because the Urban Institute finds that actual rates under the current system are much lower than they might seem in theory, it suggests that the Corman rates would result in a very large "tax" increase for working people.

Representative Al Ullman suggested that benefits should

be cut by 67 cents for each dollar of earnings in a single-parent family, after deducting $30 per month and child-care expenses. For two-parent families the rate would be 60 cents. In addition to these rates for AFDC benefits, food stamp benefits would be cut by 20 cents for each dollar earned after $30 per month and child-care expenses up to $595 per month were deducted. Above that amount, 40 cents per earned dollar would be lost. For single individuals, the rate would be 15 cents. As for the EITC, a person would receive 20 percent of the first $5,000. The EITC would be reduced by 13 cents for each dollar above $7,500.

While no calculation has been published of the actual implicit rates of the Ullman proposal as compared with the current system or the Corman bill, Ullman's staff has prepared a comparison of the nominal rates. The AFDC benefits under his plan would be reduced at rates quite similar to those currently used. The reduction rate for food stamps appears to be somewhat higher than current law, especially at higher earnings levels. In an attempt to encourage more private sector employment, Ullman has provided for a more generous EITC. Overall, the Ullman proposal seems to provide more incentives than the Corman bill, but both use considerably higher benefit reduction rates than the original Carter proposal.

Senator Long has been a persistent advocate of a work requirement rather than a work incentive. His proposal is "work for relief" and would revive the concept of the Community Work and Training Program, tried in the 1960s. All AFDC recipients with children seven years or older and anyone over 18 in an AFDC family would be required to take a job. To be sure, the "job" might not entail pay. Nonetheless, the labor performed would be considered a means of "repaying" welfare benefits received. Refusal to take such a job could result in the loss of those benefits. The program would not necessarily include training or job creation funds. The absence of such funding and of pay for work would amount to there being no incentive to work except that of qualifying for welfare. Implicitly, the Long approach is based on the belief that most welfare recipients would not otherwise be inspired to seek work and that they are content to remain on welfare.

The Baker-Bellmon bill, which essentially leaves the

current AFDC intact, would lower the benefit reduction rate somewhat by increasing the earned income disregard from $30 to $60 per month. This amount would increase to $70 in fiscal year 1985. It might also be increased in individual cases, if actual work expenses were proven to be higher. The disregarded amount is not taken into account in calculating income which causes a reduction in benefits.

Under the Baker-Bellmon proposal, the EITC would be increased from ten percent to 15 percent and would be available up to the poverty line rather than the $4,000 in current use. After the poverty level is reached, the EITC would be phased out at a 20 percent rate. It would be paid only for private sector work.

As can be seen from even this simplified explanation of the alternative approaches to providing work incentives, they are among the most complex aspects of the welfare system. In addition, they are usually discussed in terms of a model Federal system and not in the light of the varying state systems actually in use. As a result, the debate over financial work incentives is limited to those individuals and groups with sufficient expertise to develop their own projections.

The relationship between a low benefit reduction rate, a work incentive, a high breakeven point and the consequent necessity of some financial aid to relatively high-wage workers has been shown to be confusing to the general public. A 1976 Louis Harris poll found that 89 percent of the American people believe: "Too many people on welfare could be working." Only six percent of respondents disagreed. Only one year later, when questioned about the Carter proposal, 72 percent said the PBJI would "give people an incentive to work, instead of just taking government handouts." Overall, a 70 percent majority favored the plan, with only 13 percent opposed.

In determining public attitudes toward a relatively high breakeven point, much depended on the way the question was asked. "Paying cash supplements to people with incomes of $8,400 or lower in addition to the money they make from working," was opposed, 48 percent to 39 percent. At the same time respondents were asked their opinion of the proposition: "When anyone receiving direct Federal payments earned money on a job, their payments from the government would go down by

50 cents on every dollar earned, up to $8,400 in outside income, when all Federal payments would end." This statement won the support of 65 percent with only 17 percent opposed, although it implied acceptance of the same $8,400 breakeven point the sample had previously rejected.

Stockman is fearful that because of what he calls "the iron law of the breakeven point" the public will never accept a program in which the benefit reduction rate is set low enough to provide a financial incentive to work. Voters will never accept the resulting high breakeven point, he claims.

A study prepared for the Joint Economic Committee questions the work incentives of Carter's PBJI. "A father in a two-parent family with children, who refuses to work, suffers no penalty, while there is some loss in benefits for a parent in a one-parent family," the report said. "Only individuals without children lose benefits completely for refusing to accept a job. Yet since the childless individuals cannot receive created jobs, they have a lower probability of being confronted with a job." Another report prepared for the JEC downgrades the financial work incentives and claims that any improvement in incentives will result from the provision of public service jobs.

The conservative Heritage Foundation noted that if a person refuses a job, he or she does not lose all benefits, but is merely required to accept a lower level of benefits. It favors the penalty of complete removal from the welfare rolls, apparently because of substantial doubt about the effectiveness of the financial work incentive written into the PBJI.

Various mechanisms of the work incentive have come in for critical analysis. It is obvious that there are a number of disregards allowed under the Federal system and the many state systems, all of which have a major effect on the actual benefit reduction rate as opposed to the stated rate. The National Council of State Public Welfare Administrators argued that an essential part of welfare reform — necessary if some degree of simplification is to be achieved — is the establishment of single disregard allowance. The NCSPWA proposed that this allowance be set at 40 percent of gross income and should both

54

cover work-related expenses and provide a work incentive through its effect on the actual rate. The American Conservative Union was critical of disregards because they permit higher income people to receive benefits. The ACU claimed that the Carter proposal expands disregards in the current law. In addition, it suggested that child-care and other work-related expenses should be deducted from gross rather than net income so as to discourage benefits for higher income people. A confidential survey of governors by the National Governors Conference revealed a wide divergence on handling the disregard. Of the 49 responding, 12 wanted the current AFDC disregard kept, eight thought the disregard should be increased, while 18 thought it should either be decreased, limited in duration or discontinued. The remainder favored other ways of handling the matter.

The Carter PBJI calls for cash assistance benefits to be regarded as income for tax purposes. While the plan does not envisage actual collection of Federal taxes in most cases, this approach would allow the government to recover excess cash payments from people who receive welfare benefits during short periods of unemployment. The National Association of Social Workers and others strongly protested such a provision. Said the NASW: "The philosophical implications of this decision pose extremely serious threats to the established principles of social welfare policy." On the other hand, the principle of taxing benefits has long been advocated among economists and some consider the PBJI a useful first step toward this goal.

As discussed earlier, the Carter proposal provides for a waiting period during which persons expected to work are paid reduced benefits while they seek work. This mechanism is supposed to be an incentive to welfare recipients to find employment as quickly as possible. Considerable opposition has been expressed to this approach. Said the American Public Welfare Association: "It forces the family of the primary wage earner to live on approximately one-third of a poverty level income even though their fixed expenses for housing, utilities and food may exceed that amount. The important thing to note is that this 'penalty' is imposed at a time when the primary wage earner is totally dependent on the private sector — and later the public sector — to provide a job. Would it not be sufficient in-

55

centive to reduce the benefit level at the end of some period of time if the primary wage earner fails to accept employment in a private or public service job?" The Carter and Corman plans provide for an eight-week waiting period at reduced benefit levels; the Ullman proposal calls for 17 weeks.

Another element causing widespread discussion is the degree to which incentives tend to propel a welfare recipient toward private sector rather than public service jobs. The Ullman proposal explicitly favors the private sector: 1) the EITC is larger than in the Carter plan; 2) there are credits for employers who hire people off the welfare or public sector rolls; 3) there is a longer job search period and states are required to maintain payments after the end of the Federal job search phase; and 4) a bonus is provided to states which place recipients in private sector jobs.

The Urban Institute found that the Corman bill provides an undesirable incentive to take public service employment. A short five-week search period after a year of public service employment and high tax rates on earned income would encourage people to accept public jobs, because the income loss connected with waiting for such a job would be slight. In addition, the Urban Institute believes that working in a public service job would permit significant absenteeism, which would be made financially possible because of the high benefit reduction rates on any income earned from such jobs. In other words, only a lower tax rate, meaning a more sizable loss of income if the recipient were out of work, would encourage private sector employment, where absenteeism would be both less tolerated and less attractive.

In short, the notion of financial work incentives appears to be widely accepted and is likely to be found in any comprehensive welfare reform legislation. The arguments in favor of greater incentives for work in the private sector have also found a favorable response among many on Capitol Hill.

WHAT IS THE PROPER RELATIONSHIP OF FEDERAL AND STATE GOVERNMENTS?

Governments at all levels are deeply involved in the administration and financing of income maintenance programs. In fiscal year 1978, the Congressional Budget Office has estimated that, exclusive of administrative costs, the Federal government will provide $36.9 billion in aid and the states will furnish another $16.3 billion. If all Federal and state income transfer programs are counted, the total spending would be substantially higher.

As a result of this interrelationship between the Federal government and the states (and through them counties and cities), the welfare reform debate has included proposals for reducing the financial burden on states. At the same time, consideration has been given to the disparities among states and the way in which programs mesh with each other.

WHAT NEW FINANCIAL ARRANGEMENTS SHOULD BE FOUND?

The Carter Administration proposals have dealt with the financial relationship between Washington and the states through a number of programs. States will be required to supplement the basic Federal benefit, but can receive Federal help. In addition, they would generally be required to maintain their present levels of support for welfare. PBJI also would provide states protection from sharp spending increases due to the inauguration of the PBJI and would offer funds for emergency needs not met under the basic system. Similarly, states could receive assistance in handling increased administrative costs. The sum of such measures would be a degree of fiscal relief for states, but it would fall far short of the full federalization of welfare so widely sought by state officials.

Under the current welfare system, states determine welfare benefits and the Federal government provides matching funds. Because of the varying benefit levels, Federal welfare spending ranges from $300 to $1,700 per poor person.

The Carter plan turns this situation on its head. A basic Federal benefit is provided nationwide and states are given the opportunity of supplementing it. The scope of Federal assistance to help states bring the basic benefit up to the poverty line has been discussed earlier. For supplements to be eligible for Federal support, they must meet guidelines which are quite similar to those used in making the basic Federal benefit payment. And no matching fund will be available for spending on benefits above a certain level — $9,072 for a family of four. Although it is impossible to predict how many states will provide supplementation and to what degree, it seems likely that the financial provisions of the Carter plan would encourage many to do so.

If a state takes the option of handling the intake and eligibility determination functions, it would receive from 90 percent to 110 percent of its administrative costs, depending on administration accuracy achieved.

The PBJI includes "maintenance of effort" requirements for the states. States would be required to pay the Federal government ten percent of the cost of the basic benefit. Said Henry J. Aaron, Assistant HEW Secretary for Planning and Evaluation: "This requirement is designed to insure that each state maintains a financial stake in the new system, after the transition period, even if it elects not to supplement the basic Federal payment." Obviously such a stake, which might keep spending under control, is an especially helpful check on those states handling the intake function.

58

For three years, there would be a second maintenance of effort requirement. Each state would have to spend all funds allocated to it for emergency needs plus a percentage of its 1977 welfare expenditures: 90 percent in the first year, 75 percent in the second, 65 percent in the third. Actually some states might be able to spend even less, if they could still fulfill certain basic responsibilities under the law.

The PBJI would provide "hold harmless" protection for states in two different ways. In the first case, if the sum of spending on certain items exceeds a certain "effort base," the state would be repaid the amount of the excess. In the first year, the effort base would be 90 percent of current spending on AFDC, SSI, emergency assistance and general assistance plus the state's total allotment under the emergency needs program. In the next four years, the base would rise to 100 percent, 110 percent, 130 percent and 150 percent. The expenditures so protected would include the state share of the basic Federal benefit, state spending for matching supplements and for required wage supplements, the amount spent to maintain the current level of benefits for SSI recipients, 75 percent of the amount needed to "grandfather" current AFDC recipients at present benefit levels and emergency spending up to the full amount of the emergency needs allotment.

The second hold harmless provision would guarantee states a minimum amount of fiscal relief amounting to at least ten percent in the first two years and at least five percent in the third.

As mentioned earlier, there would be an emergency needs fund of $600 million nationally to allow states to provide for what HEW Secretary Califano calls "sudden and drastic changes in family circumstances." In addition to the administrative support mentioned earlier, the Carter plan would pay an amount equal to 30 percent of the basic wage in the jobs programs to cover fringe benefits and administrative responsibilities.

All of this is a complicated method of accomplishing a simple goal — providing fiscal relief to the states. According to the Center on Social Welfare Policy and Law, "the explanation of state supplementation has proven particularly confusing to welfare experts inside and outside government, and there are indications that 'clarifications' and 'simplifications' are in the works." In applying its own formulas, the Administration admitted that it is difficult to calculate the exact amount of such relief, because it depends on how states react to the new program, especially concerning supplementation. In 1981, projected as the first year of PBJI, the savings for states might be $2 billion as against what they otherwise might have spent. As people grandfathered into SSI and AFDC benefits leave the welfare rolls, the Administration claimed that savings would be even greater for the states.

The Corman Subcommittee made several changes in the supplementation and hold harmless requirements which have the net effect of substantially increasing the fiscal relief for states. As for supplementation, a different system would be used. Federal funds would be available for spending up to current AFDC plus food stamp benefit levels or the poverty level, whichever is higher, with the matching being at a rate of 75 percent up to $4,714 for a family of four and 25 percent above that amount. For the aged, blind and disabled (ABD), the Federal government would pay 25 percent of the combined current SSI plus food stamp benefits or the poverty level, whichever is higher. There would be similar matching for General Assistance payments. At the same time, states would be allowed to use a benefit reduction rate of 70 percent for supplements, instead of the 52 percent rate set for the Federal basic benefit. Thus, the states could retain a higher portion of benefits when a recipient began earning income.

A large saving is made possible by replacing the Carter plan's gradually increasing hold harmless level (the maximum limit of spending) with a permanent and lower maximum. As will be recalled, the Carter ceiling rose each of the first five years, could be further increased by inflation and was left open after the five-year period. The Corman version provided for 86 percent in the first and second years, 90 percent in the third year and 95 percent for all years after the third. According to a hypothetical calculation, a state which would have spent $100 million in 1981 under current law would spend $122 million in 1985 if the law were unchanged, $183 million under the PBJI and $95 million under Corman.

The Ullman alternative would provide for considerably less fiscal relief than either the Carter or the Cormann Subcommittee proposals. "The premise of the bill is that the states do not need $3 or $3.5 billion of fiscal relief when the unemployment rate is 4.5 percent ... or 5.2 percent. What they need is a fixed budget item, a plan whereby their cost will not grow if a recession comes along. Consequently, with an unemployment rate of 4.5 percent, fiscal relief under this plan will be very little," an Ullman staff report said.

His hold harmless formula is simply stated: states are to pay a fixed 85 percent of their 1977 cost in the future. It is, of course, impossible to calculate how much fiscal relief is embodied in the Ullman approach, because of uncertainty over the unemployment rate. The Congressional Budget Office, using a 4.5 percent rate, estimated that Corman would save $3.5 billion in fiscal year 1982. The staffs of the Joint Tax Committee and the House Ways and Means Committee came up with a saving of $1.2 billion under the Ullman plan at the same unemployment rate.

The Ullman staff explained his approach: "Under an unemployment rate of eight percent, fiscal relief under this bill will probably be substantially greater. Thus, the states have a clear choice between a plan where their costs will diminish over time, not subject to large variations due to macro-economic conditions and where there is a virtual guarantee of fiscal relief, or another proposal where the fiscal relief is much more tenuous, but is a bigger amount."

One element of the Ullman bill would cause states to return money to the Federal government. States would have to pay half the cost of errors made in benefit payments. This feature is designed to reduce their error rates. Ullman reasons that if errors are cut, administrative costs will be cut. States pay half of these as well.

The Baker-Bellmon bill would also offer fiscal relief to the states by increasing the Federal matching rate for AFDC, as outlined earlier, unless states did not take over local costs and reduce their error rates. The better the state performance on reducing errors, the nearer it would come to receiving 90 percent of its funding from the Federal government. Federal spending on Medicaid would also be increased.

While the various reform proposals all dealt with the period beginning in 1981, pressure for immediate fiscal relief has been so great that Congress has taken some action and the Carter Administration has been forced to modify its position on the pre-1981 period.

In late 1977, Congress enacted a $187 million fiscal relief bill for fiscal year 1978. This amount is to be divided among the states according to two criteria: the December 1976 AFDC expenditures and the general revenue sharing formula. The money is to be passed down to cities or counties to cover 100 percent of their AFDC spending before any of it can be used by the state. Initially, the Carter Administration had opposed interim fiscal relief, but this bill marked its concession to mounting Congressional demands. It also indicated that it would support similar legislation for later years. Projections now indicate that a like amount would be available for use in fiscal 1978 with significantly higher relief in the next two years. One projection is for $453 billion in fiscal 1979 and $523 billion in fiscal 1980. A staff member of Senator Long's Finance Committee, when asked if these amounts were to carry the states until the beginning of relief under a welfare reform act, said he "couldn't think that far ahead." It is reasonable to infer from this reaction that Senator Long is committed to fiscal relief however doubtful he might be about the provisions of any welfare reform bill.

Some of the groups testifying before Congressional committees concerned with welfare reform made it clear that they still want full Federal financing of welfare. Not surprisingly, these included organizations of state and local governments and other welfare administrators. For example, the National Association of Counties, the U.S. Conference of Mayors, the League of Cities and the American Federation of State, County and Municipal Employees argued for federalization. In its 1977 survey of governors, the National Governors Conference gave overwhelming support to full Federal financing of welfare and Medicaid. Twenty-four backed this position, while 14 opposed.

Other groups such as the National Conference of State Legislatures and the American Public Welfare Association indicated their general support for the Carter approach to the issue. It is apparent that such groups saw in the Administration's proposal the best chance for a real measure of help. Clearly, they could draw added satisfaction from the Corman amendments.

A number of spokesmen appeared to approve of the Carter proposal, but expressed doubts that it could deliver what it promised. The provision that would require states to use a 52 percent benefit reduction rate for supplementary benefits was attacked on the grounds that it would force the states to increase spending that might more than swallow the promised fiscal relief. Said New York Governor Hugh L. Carey: "It is . . . inconceivable that we could accept, under the banner of fiscal relief, the economic and fiscal consequences of a vastly expanded caseload." He went on to conclude that "only a resolution of the 52 percent problem . . . will permit the beginning of true fiscal relief . . ." By increasing the rate to 70 percent, the Corman version was designed to deal with this objection.

The National Council of State Public Welfare Administrators took much the same position. It also suggested that a more simple method should be found for grandfathering current welfare recipients. It concluded: "Despite assurance that there is at least ten percent fiscal relief for each state, we must register our concern that fiscal relief may not be as high as that projected by the Federal government, if it is there at all." The reasons for the group's pessimism were mounting Medicaid and social services costs and the failure of the Administration bill to include a cost-of-living escalator.

The representative of the U.S. Conference of Mayors and the National League of Cities was unsure that fiscal relief would be forthcoming after the first year under the Carter plan. An AFL-CIO spokesman said that the promised fiscal relief was doubtful because states would want to increase supplementation to make up for a cut in benefits resulting from the Administration approach.

There was a degree of indifference to the question of fiscal relief on the part of organizations more concerned with the recipients of welfare. One staff member of the National

Association of Social Workers said that "fiscal relief is not a significant factor" in welfare reform. He noted that it would be impossible to reduce the size of the welfare bureaucracy because of union pressure.

Richard Nathan recognized the pressing need for fiscal relief. After proposing a $4,000 Federal minimum payment, he suggested that a formula should be found to match amounts in excess of that level to "give immediate and permanent welfare fiscal relief to states and cities with high welfare burdens."

Fiscal relief was an inherent part of proposals by more conservative groups to turn welfare back to state administration to the fullest extent possible. Robert Carleson pressed for block grants to be made to states, thus allowing them to decide on how the funds should be spent. His hand guided both the U.S. Chamber of Commerce and American Conservative Union to reflect this same support for block grants and state and local control. A Chamber statement said that such grants should cover "the substantial share of the costs of public welfare programs."

Although the reasons for supporting fiscal relief may vary, there is virtually no debate about the need for providing such help to the states. In fact, the Carter Administration was the last hold-out against the interim relief successfully advocated by Senator Daniel Patrick Moynihan and others. Of course, differences over how much relief is appropriate are likely to continue to be evident in coming years.

WHO SHOULD ADMINISTER THE WELFARE SYSTEM?

Many people who speak of the "welfare mess" believe that the administration of public assistance is inefficient and that any reforms must embody considerable streamlining. Advocates of reform suggest that simplification of administration will save money without reducing benefits. Recipients of public assistance often have a different view, fearing that centralization will result in a remote, monolithic system that is unresponsive and unsympathetic to their individual needs. At the same time, welfare bureaucracies have grown up on the Federal, state and local levels. Some are efficient and some are not, but all have a vested interest in their own survival. For all these reasons, the debate over administrative reform takes on a special importance.

The Carter Administration's proposal would "make a significant change in the way that cash assistance programs are administered," according to the American Public Welfare Association. The national, uniform minimum benefit and the high degree of Federal financing would ensure effective Federal control over administration. At present, each state must designate a single state agency to administer AFDC. Some 18 states have exercised their option to pass some of their responsibilities on to local governments. Each state makes its own determination as to which agency will handle checkwriting, intake and eligibility determinations, although HEW must approve their systems. Application forms for the various programs may differ. The Federal government now proposes to take over all these functions, to have a common application form and to process information through a Federal computer system.

The Carter proposal recognizes that there will be resistance to turning the intake function over to the Federal government. As a result, it gives the states the option of handling this part of the program. In his testimony before Congressional welfare reform committees, HEW Secretary Califano said: "We recognize that states opting for state administration of the intake function have very real concerns about the responsiveness of the Federal government to the needs of their citizens ... We also recognize that, if states choose to convert to full Federal administration, the rights of their employees must be fully protected."

It is likely that the Federal government would also administer state supplementary programs so long as they generally followed Federal guidelines concerning the benefit reduction rate, filing unit and accountable period. State supplements for which there were no matching Federal funds would have to be administered by the states.

In preparing its proposal, the Carter Administration concluded that it would be unwise to put state agencies in charge of a program for which the states were not financially responsible. There are also operational benefits claimed for Federal administration. Data collection and processing, income verification and checkwriting can presumably be done more efficiently on a centralized basis. A Federal system could spot dual applications in neighboring jurisdictions. For functions such as the delivery of social services and provision of emergency assistance, the states would retain control, as they are better suited to dealing with individual problems.

The decision to ask for a shift to Federal administration also reflects the failure of HEW to induce some states to improve their administration of the AFDC program. One study showed that these states had a backlog of cases due for eligibility redetermination, a factor closely related to a high error rate. Forms are often difficult to understand. Some states use complicated eligibility rules which also increases the chances of error. Finally, state budgetary restrictions can result in changes in basic program design in an effort to conserve resources.

The bill reported out by the Corman Subcommittee on Welfare Reform departed from the original Carter proposal by offering states the option of administering all aspects of the cash assistance program. At the same time, the Corman version provided for the imposition of standards concerning promptness, the application procedure, eligibility and benefit level determination, check issuance and appeal procedures. States would have to provide applicants with a simple summary of their rights and duties under the law.

These changes reflected a desire to make the welfare system more responsive to the individual needs of recipients. But the result is an obviously more complicated system. There would be both Federal and state systems for the aged, blind and disabled. Subcommittee allowances for more specific deductions from income would make state administration more difficult. The reduction in allowable assets would require more rulings, although the subcommittee formula is simpler than the Administration proposal. States would still administer a residual food stamp program. While there are also measures to simplify administration, the net result would be greater complexity.

The Ullman alternative would keep the AFDC program and would shift all administration to the states. This decision reflects the nature of the AFDC program and apprehension that the Carter and Corman approaches to welfare reform would spur further growth of the Federal bureaucracy. The Ullman bill would require states to use the same application form for AFDC and food stamps and to coordinate information systems between the two programs.

Ullman had weighed federalized administration. "But currently and traditionally, the states have administered welfare and they are in some sense closer to the clientele," a memo published by the · Ullman staff contended. It argued that coordination was necessary between the cash and jobs components of welfare and assistance programs operated by the states. As a result, the administration of all programs affecting the poor would be brought to the state level, based on the satisfactory experience with food stamps.

Senator Russell Long, Chairman of the Senate Finance Committee, would likely line up with Ullman. An aide reported that the Senator would be "wary" of Federal administration on the basis of past experience with the SSI program.

Groups outside Congress are deeply divided on the question of Federal versus state administration. Ideological opponents on the questions of benefit levels and incremental-comprehensive reform agree in favoring state administration. In fact, there is widespread opposition to Federal control.

Not surprisingly, governors would prefer to have control shifted into their hands. The National Governors Conference survey showed that 31 of the 43 governors responding favored state administration, while ten wanted Federal responsibility and two preferred local control. Fully 38 favored the creation of a joint Federal-state team for the development and review of regulations governing welfare and Medicaid, while only one was opposed. Significant numbers, almost always a majority of respondents, indicated their feeling that changes are needed in a wide variety of administrative regulations, especially those relating to eligibility, treatment of income and work incentives. Testifying before the Cormon Subcommittee, New York Governor Carey argued for streamlined administration at the state level. Although his own state had frequently been under attack, he countered: "We come here with proof that we can administer our public assistance program according to strict standards of accountability."

The American Public Welfare Association has been most explicit in its preference for state administration. APWA spokesman Steven Minter pointed out that many state agencies would remain even if the PBJI were adopted. Coordination, he said, would be far easier with state welfare administrators than with a new Federal bureaucracy. States had already made the investment in staffs and systems capable of administering welfare. "Any nationwide cash assistance program must serve a very broad range of vulnerable people," he noted, "many of whom are for one reason or another, from time to time, in desperate straits." He argued that states have expertise and experience in this area that "is not replaceable." Minter went on at length with his contention that state welfare officials have a greater degree of responsiveness to human need than Federal officials. He also held that a dual system would needlessly be complex.

In another statement, the APWA said that those states which continue the intake function will take the brunt of criticism without being able to do much about it. The group also criticized the provisions allowing HEW to contract out administrative responsibility.

The representatives of the National Conference of State Legislatures admitted that states have varying levels of competence in administering public assistance. But he argued that Federal control would mean that the system would lose the competence and interest shown by a number of states. He also expressed concern about a dual system. "We believe that it would be possible to develop varying degrees of administrative involvement of states depending on their interest and competence without risk to the national goals of the reformed welfare system," he said. "The Federal government obviously must have the authority to determine a state's competence, but Congress should insist that the Federal government not get into administration which is duplicative and which a state is competent and willing to perform."

The National Council of State Public Welfare Administrators also went on record in favor of state administration or delegation of state responsibilities to local governments. It asked for the Federal government to assume 50 percent of the cost of administration.

State and welfare officials found themselves in line with the position of those who favor a more modest welfare reform. Richard Nathan urged that welfare reform should "move toward full state administration . . . [and] increase fiscal relief in connection with obtaining full state administration."

Similarly, Robert Carleson favored a decentralized system. In the policy statement of the American Conservative Union Welfare Reform Task Force, for which he was mainly responsible, it was argued that "a welfare system based on need and geared to provide assistance in the form of food, clothing, housing, services and work cannot be administered from Washington. It must be developed and administered at the state and local levels of government in order to tailor the assistance to meet the temporary needs of the community's truly needy in a timely and accurate manner." The report calls for giving states the right to determine eligibility, benefit levels and the form of benefits. The implication is that some states, at least, would be less generous than the Federal government.

The National Association of Social Workers testified that administration should be either wholly Federal or state, but not both. Its welfare reform task force had a great deal of difficulty deciding on its own preference, but finally agreed to come down on the side of Federal control. Yet, the task force insisted on decentralization, and a staff representative indicated that the Federal government should contract out the actual work as a means of achieving this end. For obvious reaons, NASW has also called for an assurance that employees of existing state and local programs will not be exposed to any loss of employment because of federalized administration.

The attitude of the National Association of Counties, (NACo), as initially expressed by Frank Jungas, a Minnesota official, appeared to support Federal administration. Only in the area of handling emergency assistance did the organization assert that counties would be best equipped for administrative chores. Later, however, its staff indicated that NACo was satisfied with the Corman bill, which would give states the option of assuming all administrative responsibility. A staff member noted that counties administer the welfare program in 18 states representing 60 percent of the caseload and provide social services in virtually all states.

Obviously, there is strong sentiment against the Carter Administration's proposal to shift administrative responsibility to the Federal government. The powerful coalition of opposing forces makes it appear unlikely that this provision can survive. Although the cost might be higher using state and local administration, its advocates appear to believe that the gains are commensurate with that cost.

SHOULD THE WELFARE SYSTEM PERPETUATE DIFFERENCES AMONG STATES?

One of the most profound upheavals in American history has occurred during the last 30 years. Millions have left agricultural America and crowded into the cities. Many of the newcomers, both blacks and whites, were without marketable skills or minimal educational attainments.

Mechanization of agriculture and media-induced awareness of the life offered in the cities obviously were among the factors prompting the influx. Another factor, the availability of high welfare benefits in the industrial cities and states, was also a powerful attraction.

Indeed, for many — particularly those culturally and educationally unequipped to function in urban America — welfare offered an enticing level of support. Benefits rose rapidly during the 1960s. In part, this was a natural consequence of the "War on Poverty's" drive to redistribute wealth so as to alleviate deprivation among the lowest income group.

In part, it reflected the militancy of such organizations as the National Welfare Rights Organization. Thus, in high-benefit states, such as Massachusetts, New York, Michigan or California, a welfare family of four may qualify for a total benefits package exceeding $12,000 per annum.

Obviously, millions of Americans earn far less. Former Congresswoman Martha W. Griffiths has reported on research in six major economic areas of the country. In all, a female-headed family could receive more in benefits than the average working mother with a comparably sized, dependent family might earn.

In two of the nation's six major economic areas, a welfare mother's income could exceed that of the average family's working man.

Griffiths, who headed the Subcommittee on Fiscal Policy of the Joint Economic Committee of Congress, argued that disparities between the levels of welfare benefits provided in poor and rich states necessitated equalization. She believes that the Federal government must provide a basic stipend for the entire nation. The benefit levels should be uniform. "One of the big benefits . . . of federalization and reform will be the effect of inhibiting large-scale immigration into the cities by poor people from low-benefit states," she said. "It might even be possible that some would move out. The benefit . . . then, is that you will not be paying more and more for those additional people. It should reduce the tax rates."

The Carter PBJI can be seen as meeting the objective set by Griffiths and others. It would set a basic, Federal minimum benefit rate for the entire nation. State supplementation of the Federal benefit would be possible. Where living costs or liberal social traditions prevail, such supplementation would be anticipated.

The National Association of Social Workers forecasts that PBJI would "rather dramatically" change the position of states in relation to one another. It has found that the Carter proposal's "trend . . . is toward equalization; and the equalization will be directly felt by those who now receive little or will not immediately affect those receiving higher benefits."

71

In short, while the PBJI will by its minimum standard tend to raise basic payments in the least generous states, the program will do almost nothing to encourage high-benefit states to do more than at present.

The disparities of current levels of benefits has been cited in a recent report from the Congressional Budget Office. "Benefits for a family of four in Mississippi amount to only 13 percent of the poverty threshold, while in Wisconsin they are as high as 90 percent of the threshold," the report said. The Corman Subcommittee bill and the Baker-Bellmon bill would all deal with this issue in the same way as the Carter Administration — by boosting benefits for the least favored states. The Ullman plan would carry this process to its logical conclusion by pegging Federal funds so as to have benefit levels in all states ultimately reach an amount equal to 30 percent of median state personal income.

In order to achieve the objective of greater equalization, more Federal aid must go to those states and cities where benefits are low. "According to its own estimates, the Administration's bill will redistribute the nation's income away from northern and western to southern states," Senator Moynihan told the House Welfare Reform Subcommittee. HEW Secretary Califano admitted this analysis was correct in a table he submitted in answer to a question from the subcommittee on the flow on Federal funds:

	Pre-reform Federal Cash	Pre-reform CETA+	Post-reform Federal Cash	Post-reform Jobs+Cash
Northeast	23.1%	24.7%	23.0%	22.6%
North Central	22.7%	22.9%	21.9%	22.7%
South	36.4%	33.6%	38.4%	38.1%
West	17.8%	18.7%	16.7%	16.6%

Changes between the second and fourth columns in particular raised the ire of representatives of the regions which would lose. They felt that, in fact, their states were being penalized for having made the best effort prior to reform.

Several groups argued that the welfare reform plans failed to take into account regional cost-of-living differences.

The Welfare Debate of 1978

Speaking on behalf of the Northeast-Midwest Economic Advancement Coalition, composed of 204 House members, New York Representative Charles B. Rangel, a leader in the Congress' Black Caucus, said ". . . the Federal share of the new welfare reform proposal would not provide an equal amount of purchasing power across the states, leaving a number of states, primarily in the Northeast and Midwest to bear the brunt of regional cost differences." A Coalition report also noted that high-benefit states would actually end up reimbursing recipients for Federal income taxes they might have to pay as a result of the Carter plan. It criticized the flat $150 child-care deduction and the 30 percent allowance for overhead in the public service jobs program for failing to reflect regional differences.

An analysis of the Carter plan by the Urban Institute presented the opposing viewpoint. "A system that varied benefit amounts among all states based on a cost-of-living index [advocated by the Coalition] would introduce added administrative complexity for little gain in conforming benefit amounts to actual need," the report said. "If adjustments were made on a state-to-state basis, huge intrastate price differentials would be hidden." The Urban Institute also noted that existing variations among the states were due more to different priorities than to different cost-of-living determinations.

Because the Carter plan was designed to boost the lowest state benefit levels, some of those cities with the greatest economic privation get the least help. Hartford City Council President Nicholas Carbone, speaking on behalf of the U.S. Conference of Mayors and the National League of Cities, said that "16 of the top 20 'hardship cities' [as defined by a Brookings Institution study] are located in states which stand to gain the least under the Administration's 'reform' system. Yet, these are the very states which bear the greatest welfare burden." A study by the American Federation of State, County and Municipal Employees found that Federal aid to Wyoming would increase by 147.5 percent, but New York, which has three of the 20 hardship cities, would get only a 5.3 percent increase, placing it 45th in terms of additional Federal aid. The AFSCME study also claimed that the jobs portion of the PBJI would be funded out of cutbacks in CETA which would especially

73

penalize these same 20 cities where a large part of the city work force is now supported by CETA.

The Northeast-Midwest Coalition found other examples of what it felt to be discrimination against the regions it represents. "Because of inequities inherent in the Medicaid and AFDC formula," its report said, "the Coalition states tend to be reimbursed at lower percentage rates than are states in the South and West." Yet another concern was the Administration plan to finance some of the added costs of reform out of the intended proceeds of the wellhead tax, part of the energy bill. Because this tax would, if enacted, drive up fuel prices in the Coalition states, it was argued that it should be rebated directly to consumers there. If it were allocated to the national welfare program, the net result would be increased energy costs in the Coalition states.

Although it is unlikely that the Coalition states would support the welfare reform concepts of conservative groups, notably those of the U.S. Chamber of Commerce and the American Conservative Union, their proposal for providing block grants to the states and letting each determine its own welfare program was, in theory at least, the most effective way of meeting the Coalition's objections. Of course, the Coalition states would fear that the amount received under such an approach would be inadequate and would force them either to reduce benefits or spend more of their own resources.

Although the impact of a Federal jobs program on migration is difficult to determine, an official of the NASW contended that "people don't move to seek higher pay or payments, but they do move to seek jobs. This is especially significant if jobs are not created in rural areas." Many believe that it would be far more difficult to create public service jobs in rural areas, under the PBJI, than in cities.

One clear-cut way to accomplish the benefit equalization objectives of the various welfare reform plans and to meet the financial needs of states with the greatest welfare problem would be to set a national standard at a relatively high level. But the cost implications of such a policy virtually insure that it would not be adopted. It remains to be seen if members of Congress from Coalition states will allow their dissatisfaction with what they feel is discrimination against their states to carry them to the point of opposing major welfare reform proposals.

HOW SHOULD WELFARE RELATE TO MEDICAID AND OTHER PROGRAMS?

"The real mess," according to Richard P. Nathan, "is not welfare — but Medicaid."

Yet the Carter proposal, the Corman version, the Ullman alternative and the Baker-Bellmon bill all avoided the issue of reforming Medicaid. All seemed to accept the premise that welfare reform means income maintenance alone and not other parts of the public welfare system.

To be sure, President Carter is likely to propose national health insurance legislation, which if enacted, would presumably resolve the Medicaid issue. Even so, there is a potentially complicating factor: under the current welfare system, those receiving AFDC and SSI also automatically receive Medicaid. If PBJI were enacted, the number of people receiving welfare benefits would be significantly expanded. It would, therefore, be very difficult to extend Medicaid benefits to them on the same automatic basis as at present. As it is, Medicaid costs have soared in recent years. Automatic Medicaid coverage for everybody under PBJI could "break the bank." So the Carter proposal merely provided that states would have to provide Medicaid to those people who met current eligibility requirements associated with AFDC and SSI. In addition, those states which have already opened Medicaid to people not eligible for cash assistance, might continue to do so, providing Medicaid to people with incomes up to 33 percent above the cash benefit level.

The Carter approach has received some support, mostly from those who are optimistic about early action on national health insurance. In testifying before the House Welfare Subcommittee, Melvin Glasser, head of the UAW's Social Security Department, expressed concern that states would try to stem rising Medicaid costs by restricting benefits and eligibility. As a result, he advocated maintenance of the status quo, much as the Carter bill has done.

Considerable opposition has been expressed by those who fear administrative snarls and continued rising costs. A study by the Joint Economic Committee suggests that enacting welfare reform, while deferring action on Medicaid, could result in a serious problem of benefit reduction rates. The situation would arise because of the "uneven" interaction of welfare and other programs. For example, the American Public Welfare Association has asked: "Will minimum wage jobs raise people to an income level in certain states [at which] they no longer can receive Medicaid? If so, there could be a situation in which some families are better off in cash terms, but, in absolute terms, the loss of Medicaid could more than offset the gain in cash." The APWA also argued that for those not expected to work, but who would like to find a job, the loss of Medicaid would be a strong disincentive.

Several groups suggest that the Carter proposal will actually stimulate demand for Medicaid. The National Council of State Public Welfare Administrators believes that "states will surely face additional Medicaid costs simply because of the increased rate of participation expected in the new program." In other words, because the PBJI will make many already potentially eligible for AFDC aware of their right to benefits, the Medicaid rolls will inevitably grow.

Both the NCSPWA and the National Conference of State Legislatures worry that the courts will not allow the distinction between those people under PBJI who are eligible for Medicaid and those who are not. Said Connecticut State Representative Irving Stolberg on behalf of the NCSL, "Court challenges raising equal protection arguments are likely to force states to provide identical treatment to the new recipients and classes covered by the reformed welfare system . . . The political and equity arguments for extending coverage for medical assistance are hard to refute," he said, "and, consequently, enormous pressures on the legislatures will likely occur . . . To have to extend Medicaid coverage to large numbers of new recipients would be disastrous and would consume any fiscal relief that states hope to gain by the new welfare reform program."

Both groups want protection against rising costs resulting from any court decision or Federal action which requires them to extend Medicaid coverage. They both recognize that the danger of such rising costs will be an incentive to Congress to act rapidly on national health insurance.

In addition to potential growth in the number of recipients, the administration of Medicaid will become more cumbersome. States will have to determine eligibility separately for PBJI and for Medicaid. As a result, states can expect increased administrative costs. They have asked for Federal financing of the added expenditures resulting from operating two different eligibility systems. The Corman bill met this request by promising to hold states harmless for such added costs.

For some groups, such palliatives are not enough. The American Public Welfare Association is pessimistic about the chances for the early adoption of national health insurance. While the APWA is sympathetic to the Administration's view, Steven Minter, its president, told the House Welfare Reform Subcommittee, "we believe . . . that the relationship of Medicaid to the jobs and income program is so vital that we urge the Administration and Congress to address the complex relationships between the programs and to fully explore the impact various approaches would have on the poor." The NCSL is more explicit and calls for extending Medicaid to new recipients with full funding provided by the Federal government. The National Association of Social Workers also wants Medicaid extended to all covered under the PBJI.

Because of the Carter plan's emphasis on income maintenance, it has been criticized for not being sufficiently well coordinated with other social services. Critics believe that, just as has happened in the case of Medicaid, welfare reform will increase the demand for social services as more people receive public assistance. Yet, the bill contains no additional money for social services.

Attention has also been focused on child care. While the Carter proposal placed some emphasis on single parents — usually mothers — taking jobs, it does not seem to recognize arguments on behalf of additional day-care programs. Said

Carol Parry, of the New York City Department of Social Services, who testified on behalf of the NASW, "The welfare proposal creates the double bind of requiring some mothers to work (three out of eight at current estimates), but makes no provision for their children either in terms of an equitable allowance or available facilities. A true reform of the welfare system must include, both quantitatively and qualitatively, an adequate child-care program." The NCSPWA also advocated stepped-up funding for social services including child care.

The APWA also noted the lack of coordination between the PBJI and foster-care plans operated by the states. The Administration had indicated that this problem is covered in other pending legislation and has promised to alter the welfare reform proposal if that bill does not pass. In addition the APWA pointed out that if states choose to allow the Federal government to handle administrative aspects of income maintenance, they will continue to be responsible for social services. The result would be a glaring lack of coordination between the cash assistance program and social services.

In short, critics understand and even somewhat sympathize with the Administration's reasoning in separating Medicaid and social services from income maintenance. Yet, many believe that such a separation actually undermines the effectiveness of many of the intended reforms. As a result, they urge immediate attention to coordinating Medicaid and social service with the PBJI, even though it would make the overall program more costly. They want this cost to be borne by the Federal government.

SHOULD FOOD STAMPS BE CASHED OUT?

The food stamp program has been the only Federal program providing benefits to all poor people. As such, it establishes, in effect, a floor under the incomes of people who are not eligible for cash aid. As a Federal program, it has tended to reduce the differences among states resulting from varying AFDC and SSI payments. In recent years, people who became unemployed but who were not eligible for welfare payments were greatly helped by the availability of food stamps. Given its wide availability and uniform eligibility standards, the food stamp program could be said to have served as the first step toward a consolidated cash welfare reform.

Some of the most generous features of the food stamp program, resulting from eligibility requirements that looked mainly at income levels, have been criticized. So has the failure of the program to reach all who might be in need. As a result, the program has been subject to Congressional review and has been modified four times in the past seven years.

The most recent modification, in 1977, eliminated the requirement that recipients pay cash for their coupons. This provision had originally been used as a way of obliging recipients to allocate about 30 percent of their income to food purchases. As income rose, a recipient had to pay more for stamps. But only about 50 percent of those eligible for food stamps participated. The others refrained principally because they could not accumulate sufficient cash to pay for the stamps. According to HEW Secretary Califano, the 1977 law could ultimately have the effect of enabling about three million more people to join those eligible for food stamps. The Agriculture Department figured the average number of participants during any month in 1976 to be 18.5 million.

At the same time, eligibility and fraud provisions were

tightened so as to eliminate some 1.3 million people from the program. Participants cannot have a net income above the poverty line. The law also makes it more difficult for students to obtain food stamps. And, in recognition of the influence of work-fare proponents, a number of experimental projects were begun in which recipients could work off the value of their food stamps. Finally, the assets test was tightened. Thus, for example, those with expensive automobiles would not be able to receive stamps.

By terminating the automatic eligibility of welfare recipients and imposing the poverty line ceiling, Congress stripped the program of some of its most controversial features. Nonetheless, food stamps, which still have a relatively low benefit reduction rate and high breakeven point, remain as the nearest thing to a national minimum benefit.

Just as these reforms were being set in place, the Carter Administration proposed, as part of its PBJI welfare reform, that food stamps should be cashed out. Welfare recipients should receive the cash value of food stamps and would, of course, have complete discretion over how the money was spent. The value of food stamps would simply become part of the minimum Federal benefit payment.

A number of arguments in favor of the cash-out were considered. A report by the Congressional Budget Office found that "because poor families, with or without assistance, spend most of their limited funds on food and housing, the effect of the food stamp and housing assistance programs is more one of general income supplementation than increased food or shelter consumption." The CBO contrasted this finding with its belief that without an in-kind medical services benefit, poor people would spend less on health care. A Brookings Institution report said that "for most recipients, food stamps, in fact, are little different in their effect than a cash payment since they increase expenditures for food by, at most, 15 or 20 cents per dollar of benefits compared to the payment of the cash equivalent." The report suggested that half of the value of stamps goes toward added spending on food with the rest merely freeing cash that would have been spent on food for other purposes. About one-third of an equivalent cash payment would be spent on added food purchases, according to the report.

Both the CBO and Brookings reports find that there is no evidence that food stamps improve nutrition. Recipients can purchase whatever foods they wish, and there are no findings that they pay more attention to nutrition when they use stamps than when they use cash.

An Urban Institute report enumerated other arguments in favor of cash rather than stamps. Stamps deny recipients budgetary flexibility. The report noted than an AFDC mother of three in Mississippi finds that 77 percent of her total benefits are earmarked for food, while a similar recipient in New York only spends 15 percent of benefits for food. At present, AFDC and food stamps are governed by different rules which could be replaced by a simpler, single mechanism, according to the Urban Institute. Others have pointed out that the sheer cost of printing, distributing and redeeming stamps could be saved. The differing food stamp and welfare programs usually impose a burden on recipients who must go to separate offices to obtain benefits.

Food stamps constitute a second currency, according to the Urban Institute. A black market in food stamps, where those in excess of family needs are turned into cash, has existed. In addition, some people, particularly the elderly, are embarrassed to use this alternative form of payment. Some recipients consider food stamps a form of paternalism and feel that their dignity is undermined by having to use them. The Urban Institute suggested that the lower participation rate of eligible people in the food stamp program as compared with AFDC may result from this sentiment.

Undoubtedly, the principal reason for the Administration's proposal to convert stamps to cash is found in the Brookings study: "Because of its universal coverage, cashing out the food stamp program implies instituting a comprehensive cash assistance program. Such a step neither should nor probably would be taken except in conjunction with total reform of the welfare system." It was just such a reform that Carter had in mind.

HEW Secretary Califano has estimated that about three million people now able to acquire food stamps would lose

81

eligibility for public assistance if food stamps were cashed out. "The major reasons for this loss of eligibility are the longer accountability period and the higher tax rate on unearned income," he said. In other words, many of the unemployed who are now not eligible for welfare would lose their existing eligibility for food stamps. He adds that of the three million losing eligibility, only one million actually participate in the program.

When the Corman Subcommittee considered cashing out food stamps, it voted to go along with the Administration proposal. However, it was concerned about the potential loss of eligibility would lower the benefit reduction rate for incomes below $7.500 and increase it for incomes above that level. He also proposed a number of adjustments in allowable deductions from the amount of income that is taken into consideration and a minimum benefit of $10 in food stamps for all household units. allowed in the reformed welfare system. A preliminary Department of Agriculture estimate showed that about one million people (five percent of current recipients) would participate in the residual food stamp program. In contrast with the Carter proposal, the Corman version would provide for disregarding the cash value of food stamps in computing benefits under other Federal means-tested aid programs.

The alternative reform package by House Ways and Means Chairman Al Ullman would not cash out food stamps. Under its provisions, the cash payment would be the same for all filing units; only the food stamps would vary according to the number of people in the family. "Food stamps remain a basic element in the bill," said Ullman. "I don't agree that food stamps are demeaning or presumptuous. Food stamps are one way this nation feeds its own people in economic distress. The program works. And it should be continued." To allow for administrative simplification and because food stamps are supposed to mesh with cash benefits, Ullman proposed that rules for AFDC and food stamps be uniform, with a single application form. Uniform eligibility would lower the benefit reduction rate for incomes below $7,500 and increase it for incomes above that level. He also proposed a number of adjustments in allowable deductions from the amount of income that is taken into consideration and a minimum benefit of $10 in food stamps for all household units.

In a paper accompanying the Ullman proposal, his staff contended that provision of food stamps is important in that they assure that tax dollars actually bring the desired result — feeding the poor.

The staff paper also addressed "the argument ... that cash assistance is cheaper to the taxpayer since it requires much lower overhead expense: eight to nine percent for AFDC and SSI compared to 15 percent for food stamps." The Ullman staff maintained that benefits are smaller per unit under food stamps because it is mainly a supplementary program for the working poor rather than a basic assistance program. In addition recipients are required to file monthly reports, thus increasing administrative costs. Actually, "For each application, food stamps spends roughly $180 while AFDC spends $250 on administrative cost," the paper said. "The Ullman plan will reduce administrative costs in both programs because it standardizes many of the components of eligibility," the staff reported. The Baker-Bellmon bill would make no change in the current food stamp program, although it would authorize a test of cashing them out.

Because of the proposal to cash out food stamps, the welfare reform debate extended to the Agriculture Committee in both the House and Senate. On the House side, Representative Thomas Foley, the Agriculture Committee chairman, has been outspokenly in favor of keeping food stamps. A committee aide said that there had been no pressure from producers or food stores to keep food stamps, an indication that they are not worried about a loss of sales. But the aide indicated that after all the efforts at reform of the food stamp program, the committee would like to see it in full operation, not immediately replaced. In rebuttal, the Urban Institute noted that the welfare reform plan would not go into effect until fiscal year 1981, so that during the interim, the 1977 food stamp reform program would be used. In addition, Foley favored an incremental approach to welfare reform, and defined it to mean that, in the absence of a comprehensive cash system, food stamps would have to be retained.

Opinion on the Agriculture Committee appeared to be

divided. Some members shared Foley's concern about diminishing the committee's jurisdiction by abolishing food stamps. They also believed that food stamps reach the poor more efficiently than cash assistance. It has been calculated that about 45 cents of each dollar in the Carter proposal goes to poor people as opposed to those above the poverty line. In contrast, perhaps as much as 90 percent of funds appropriated for food stamps actually go to the poor. Liberals in this group had also hoped that, if food stamps were saved, they could serve as a supplement to the $4,200 basic payment, but this hope has dissipated.

On the Senate side, neither Agriculture Committee Chairman Herman Talmadge nor Nutrition Subcommitee Chairman George McGovern indicated their views on food stamps, although it may be expected that they would continue to support the program. A committee aide said that the key question is whether or not the proposal is better from a poor person's viewpoint. "Cashing out food stamps was a good idea when Nixon proposed it," he said, "but the situation has changed." He suggested that the combined low benefit reduction rate of Federal food stamps and the generally higher AFDC state rates meshed together well. He also worried about the elimination of one million current recipients. Addressing the charge that food stamps are demeaning, he noted that the problem only exists in the relatively few areas where food stamp recipients and non-recipients both do their shopping in the same stores. The trade-off in terms of the positive aspects of food stamps might make this drawback acceptable. He also suggested that once food stamps were cashed out demand might grow again for a supplementary food program if nutrition levels fell. He thought that a commodity program rather than food stamps might make a comeback in this case. Although skeptical of the cash-out's effects, he concluded that "we wouldn't fight the end of food stamps if a new program gave more to the poor."

Some interest groups chose to remain aloof from the debate because their concerns lie elsewhere. But there was a sharp division of opinion among groups taking a position on the proposed cash-out.

The American Public Welfare Association, the National Council of State Public Welfare Administrators, the National Association of Counties and the National Governors Conference argued, in the words of a representative of the governors, that it is "inappropriate for government to dictate how citizens spend their money."

Some groups like the idea of cashing out food stamps, but oppose doing it now. In his testimony before the House Subcommittee, Urban League official Ronald Brown said that "while favoring cash over in-kind benefits, the Urban League believes that many reasons justify the continued use of certain in-kind benefits, e.g., when cash assistance is not adequate to meet minimum consumption needs; when the service being provided is extremely expensive (but greatly needed); when the service is scarce, does not respond to free-market forces and has a basic social utility." Although it might be argued that food stamps do not fit the exceptions outlined, an Urban League aide indicated that the group does not favor abolishing food stamps.

The UAW spokesman at the House hearings said his union supports "the goal" of cashing out food stamps. "But the precipitous manner of doing so is bound to create additional hardships for the poor," he said. "The program should be continued at least until cash benefits are comparable to the poverty level. And even then, consideration should be given to continuation of a sharply reduced emergency assistance plan to provide benefits while eligibility for cash benefits is being established."

"We are vigorously opposed to abolishing the food stamp program," said the AFL-CIO's Bert Seidman in testimony before the House panel. The union's opposition was based on its belief that the working poor should not be required to resort to welfare when they are forced into unemployment.

Some spokesmen for conservative organizations questioned the advisability of cashing out food stamps. While "consolidation could lead to a much simpler administration with less chance of fraud and error, less bureaucratic maladministration, and much more simplicity," said a Heritage Foundation report, " . . . even here caution should be exercised. It should be recalled that one reason why the food stamp program was designed as an in-kind benefit plan was that it was felt by many that poor people who received cash benefits would not spend them for food, but on other goods which were often luxury items or completely unnecessary (e.g., liquor or television) . . . If there is widespread misuse of the money, it is likely to be the children of the poor who suffer most."

In its welfare policy statement, the American Conservative Union expressed the concern that cash payments, as opposed to in-kind benefits, will remove the incentive for people to look for work. "For the able-bodied, for the period when no work is available, assistance should be in the form of food (or food stamps), clothing, housing and necessary medical and other services. Cash should go only to those who are working; in the form of wages for time worked."

The issue of cashing-out food stamps lies at the heart of the debate over a shift to a comprehensive cash welfare system. It is fair to say that without the cash-out of food stamps, the idea of comprehensive rather than incremental reform falls. Thus, the demonstrated support for food stamps of the two Agriculture committees may well constitute a long-term obstacle to comprehensive reform.

HOW MUCH DOES
WELFARE REFORM COST?

One of the major arguments of the incrementalists is that, while certain reforms may be socially desirable, they would drive the total cost of welfare so high as to make it politically undesirable. As a result, they favor removing elements from the reform package until the point is reached where the cost is acceptable. During the debates in the Corman Subcommittee, those who supported the Ullman incremental alternative most often cited its purportedly lower cost as its most attractive characteristic.

By August 1977, when the Administration submitted its comprehensive welfare reform proposal, it was forced to admit that it would cost more than the current system. The gross added costs of the Carter plan were set at $31.1 billion. The new employment programs would cost $8.8 billion; cash assistance, $20.2 billion; the EITC, $1.5 billion; and the emergency assistance program, $600 million. But from this total would be deducted a number of offsets.

Elimination of AFDC	$6.4 billion
Elimination of SSI	5.7
Reduction in food stamps	5.5
EITC	1.1
Cutting extended unemployment insurance	.7
CETA cuts	5.5
WIN program cuts	.4
Increased FICA tax	.7
Reduced unemployment insurance demand	.3
Reduced HUD program demand	.3
Fraud control savings	.4
Wellhead tax proceeds	1.3
	$28.3 billion

It is important to note that this estimate was calculated in 1978 dollars, although the PBJI would not have come fully into effect until fiscal year 1982. At that time, due to the effect of inflation, the numbers might well be substantially higher.

Some of the gains — the offsets noted above — would be the result of replacing current welfare benefits with the minimum cash payment. Other supposed savings impressed some as rather illusory. For instance, the claimed increase in revenues from the FICA tax (Social Security withholding) will occur whether or not there is welfare reform. Similar questions arose over claims of savings to be achieved through PBJI fraud control savings. In fact, HEW was already claiming that it was reducing fraud. The wellhead tax rebate related to the pending energy bill, not welfare reform. Because the wellhead tax could be expected to be passed on to consumers, that bill provided for a rebate. The energy plan proposed that the rebate also go to "the poor who do not pay taxes." The allocation in the welfare reform proposal represented $45 per person for those not paying taxes. It could be argued that, if welfare reform were not adopted, but the energy bill passed, such a rebate should have been paid in any case so as to cover higher energy costs. In that light, the wellhead tax could hardly be counted as a saving. Finally, in regard to the $3 billion that would go to middle-income taxpayers as a result of the EITC, the Administration categorized it as a part of tax reform rather than as welfare reform.

The original Administration cost estimate came in for some sharp criticism. The American Public Welfare Association reported that "many welfare policy analysts are incredulous over the cost estimates provided." It argued that "the Administration arrived at the figure of $2.0 billion additional Federal cost not by comparing the cost of the current programs alone with the anticipated cost of the new program, but by adding several other 'offsets' which cannot fairly be described as costs of the current welfare system." It questioned the inclusion of the economic stimulus portions of CETA and WIN, the wellhead tax revenues and the fraud savings. What the inclusion of savings and revenues that should be properly allocated to Social Security and Unemployment Insurance signifies, APWA said, "is that $8 billion to $9 billion, or more, is being put into a new welfare system above the amount currently spent on what we call 'welfare.' "

Opposition from the conservative end of the political spectrum sounded much the same. The American Conservative Union claimed that "the cost estimates have been seriously understated." An analysis by the Heritage Foundation came up with findings remarkably similar to those of the APWA. It estimated an added $8.6 billion should be counted when the amount of increased spending over the current welfare system is calculated. In addition, it suggested that Medicaid costs would rise and that the hold harmless provision would encourage states to increase their own welfare spending just before the reform went into effect in the knowledge that the Federal government would have to foot the bill. The Foundation also concluded that it is "proper to greet with skepticism the Administration's estimate of an increase of only two million more cash recipients." When it took all factors into account, the Heritage Foundation claimed that the Carter package would cost a total of $17.8 billion more than the current system.

In November 1977, the CBO produced its first estimate of the net cost of the Carter proposal. It had used a number of premises that differed markedly from those used in the Administration's cost determinations. Thus, CBO used 1982 dollars and projected the cost for that fiscal year. It assumed a 4.5 percent unemployment rate, while the Administration had used a 5.6 percent rate. As for the planned discontinuation of CETA's stimulative program and extended Unemployment Insurance, to say nothing of the wellhead tax, CBO said that it could not count these as savings because it did not project them as being in effect in 1982.

The net result of the initial CBO calculation was that the Carter program would entail an increased Federal cost of $13.97 billion. About $4.26 billion of this amount was Federal fiscal relief to the states. The original HEW figures had not included any express mention of how fiscal relief had been taken into account.

The Urban Institute found that, while the cost estimates of HEW and the CBO appeared to be quite different, "a careful analysis of the components reveals that the estimates are remarkably similar when allowance is made for the four-year difference in the costs to be attributed to welfare reform." The CBO had made a number of assumptions about the public jobs program, including at least one that was a mistaken interpretation of HEW's meaning.

Even if it were possible to say that the original HEW estimate (which had been subject to serious attack) was not too far from the first CBO estimate, once some of the most contentious points were eliminated and effect of inflation was added, there would still be a serious problem with the Carter figure on political grounds. By using 1978 dollars for a 1982 program, the Administration left itself open to charges that it had used sleight-of-hand to give the impression that added cost was less than it really would be. The effect of the uncertainty about the Administration figures was to undermine the credibility of its position in the debate over cost.

In January 1978, there was another exchange between HEW and the CBO. The Congressional office took the opportunity to revise its original estimate on the basis of improved techniques. The Administration restated its cost estimate in the 1979 Budget. CBO thus could make an entirely new comparison.

The most important CBO conclusion was that net Federal costs would rise by about $17.36 billion, some $3.39 billion more than in its previous estimate. The portion of this sum that would take the form of fiscal relief would decline somewhat to $3.42 billion.

Most of the reason for the widening gap was CBO's lowered expectations on offsets. It found that receipts from income and Social Security taxes would be far less than it had anticipated. Because it had used the same economic assumptions as in its earlier report, it is not clear why the CBO felt it necessary to alter its projections of tax receipts. On the spending side, the CBO found changes in the amounts for basic cash assistance, public service employment and overhead which had the net effect of a $1.43 billion increase.

At the same time that the CBO was increasing its estimate, so was the Administration. For the first time, HEW provided figures for fiscal 1982. Just the same, the CBO cost estimate was $8.6 billion higher than the Administration's figure of $8.8 billion.

On the gross cost side of the ledger, the CBO estimate was $3.5 billion higher, mostly because of the use of different economic and demographic assumptions, different techniques and data bases and divergent views of the income tax structure four years hence. The even wider gap on the offset side — the CBO was $5.1 billion lower — reflected continuing differences about what should be counted as an offset to increased welfare spending. The Administration had, in effect, refused to give ground to its critics on such matters as CETA, the wellhead tax and fraud control.

Once the new CBO report was made, it became clear that its figures, rather than the ones used in the Federal budget, would be generally accepted. The reasons seemed simple — its offset determinations were more in line with Congressional opinion and the net result was a higher figure. The Carter plan, priced by CBO at an added $17.36 billion, was obviously an easier target.

In March 1978, the CBO provided cost estimates for the Corman Subcommittee version of the bill. Although the subcommittee had been aware that its proposals were driving up the total costs, it had not placed price tags on its changes.

The CBO found that the Corman bill would cost the Federal government $20.22 billion, some $4.08 billion more than the Administration bill. A major factor in the difference was the more generous basic cash assistance program. Some 45 percent of the estimated difference between the Corman and Carter versions was due to the inclusion, in the subcommittee bill, of a cost-of-living index for years after fiscal year 1981. Other major contributing factors were increased eligibility for benefits resulting from a one-month rather than a six-month accounting period and the reduction in work effort resulting from increased benefits.

During the course of the debate on indexing benefits, Carter Administration officials went beyond the position they had appeared to hold in originally submitting cost estimates. They had suggested at first that benefits would be indexed from the 1978 figures they submitted until fiscal year 1981, when the reforms took effect. It appeared that they wished to leave to Congress the responsibility for increasing benefits as the cost of living rose in 1982 and later years. Then, the Administration said that it would not want real benefits to be eaten away by inflation. When the CBO calculated the relative costs of the Carter and Corman plans, with both being indexed, it concluded that the subcommittee's bill would result in Federal costs $1.08 billion higher than that of the Carter proposal. Seen in this light, the Corman version represents a relatively small change in the original proposal. The subcommittee's additional spending, with the exception of indexing, is largely offset by its decision to tax cash assistance.

It is extremely important to recognize, however, that the March CBO estimate of the Corman version did not include the cost of several decisions. Each would drive up the total cost of the program. Because of lack of sufficient data, the CBO did not price the decision not to repeal food stamps, the provision that benefits would not be reduced during the job search period in areas with substantial unemployment and a host of administrative changes. If these computations had been made, the Corman version would, obviously, be much more expensive than Carter's PBJI.

Another element was added to the debate when the Joint Economic Committee published a cost analysis of the Carter proposal, using the Administration's own original cost estimate as its base. This study did not recalculate the cost of the entire program. Instead it studied the cost impact of certain specific changes that might be made in the original proposal. Here are some of the study's conclusions:

PROGRAM CHANGE	ADDED (DECREASED) COST
Replace 2 tiers with one	$0.4 billion
Keeping EITC unchanged	(3.8)
Eliminating EITC	(3.9)
Lower cash benefits for those taking public service employment	(1.6)
Increasing wage from minimum to $3/hr.	2.6

Increasing wage from minimum to $4/hr.	$15.3 billion
Make public service job available to one wage earner in each household	37.0
Put 800,000 job ceiling on PBJI jobs	(2.0)
Eliminate Federal support for state supplementation and use funds to increase basic cash payments	1.6

The Ullman alternative, presented just before the Corman Subcommittee was to vote on its version of welfare reform, relied on the staffs of the Joint Tax Committee and the House Ways and Means Committee for cost estimates. They claimed that they had used methods similar to the CBO. To a certain extent, their task was easier, because they were dealing with changes to existing programs.

The cost estimate in fiscal 1982 for the Ullman plan was set at about $8 to $9 billion above current costs, considerably less than the Corman or Carter plans. Ullman suggested six reasons for the difference:

1. Less fiscal relief in Ullman plan.
2. Smaller jobs program in Ullman, costing $4 billion less.
3. $1.5 billion less for administering the jobs program.
4. Ullman recoups benefits from higher income families.
5. Ullman taxes unemployment insurance.
6. Ullman claims superior error control.

As was noted earlier, if unemployment were significantly higher, the Ullman plan could turn out to be more costly than the other two. The Ullman formula for keeping up with inflation is somewhat complicated. Benefits are to be increased to reflect inflation up to a target Federal benefit level which is 30 percent of the 1975 state median family income, itself adjusted for inflation. Presumably the 1982 Ullman figures reflect this formula's effect up to that year.

While finishing touches were still being put on the Baker-Bellmon proposal, drafts were sent to CBO for their cost estimate. The Congressional office found that the bill would add

$9.33 billion to Federal outlays in fiscal year 1982. Among the major reasons why this proposal appears to be less costly than the Carter or Corman plans are the lower price tag on the public service employment element and the job voucher program as compared with a broader jobs program, the lack of any estimate for the job tax credit and a smaller allocation for emergency assistance.

The CBO estimate of added Baker-Bellmon costs did not include figures reflecting the impact of the job tax credit on business taxes, although the Congressional agency said that a similar proposal made by Senator Baker earlier would have resulted in a revenue loss of $1.9 billion. Offsetting savings in the AFDC-Unemployed Parent program were also not estimated. The CBO did not take into account a revision in the bill which would have denied benefits to many with incomes over $10,000. Nor did the estimate reflect increased tax receipts from newly employed people. In addition, Senator Bellmon's staff challenged some of the CBO's assumptions, claiming they resulted in an unnecessarily high total. The staff came up with a Federal cost of $7.83 billion.

The lower price tag was the most obviously attractive part of the Ullman and Baker-Bellmon proposals and represented the strongest case in Congress for the incremental approach. But even these plans called for a sizeable increase in the amount of Federal spending on welfare. In fact, more than either of the other two plans, they reflect the recognition that, in the absence' of spending cuts in Federal income transfer programs, even modest welfare reform will cost more money.

One of the starting points in the debate over welfare reform was that the program cost too much, presumably because of a bloated bureaucracy and extensive cheating. Unfortunately, neither Congress nor the President has proposed a method that would significantly reduce the welfare bureaucracy. As for fraud, the Administration has produced the first indications that the most obvious kinds of cheating are being eliminated. However, in a complex program of this size, a certain percentage of errors is inevitable. The Carter Administration claimed that, since the welfare system is currently run mainly by the states, high error rates are the fault of those states which have weak operations. Clearly, some improvement is possible, especially if the system is simplified. But Congress appeared to believe that error reduction will not result in major savings. Only those who oppose any increase in welfare benefits or advocate an actual rollback claim that cutting errors will result in a lower total program cost.

It is noteworthy that the AFL-CIO, in whose ranks are millions of taxpayers who must bear the burden of increased welfare costs, supported higher wage payments under the jobs program and more adequate benefits. These can be quite costly, as the JEC study indicated. And the study did not indicate the cost of bringing the welfare payments up to the poverty level nationally. An AFL-CIO spokesman claimed that union members would be willing to bear the additional cost burden because it would only represent a transitional financial responsibility. If people were given reasonably good jobs and those on welfare were able to live at reasonably respectable levels, he argued, the United States would begin moving toward a clear reduction in the absolute numbers of people requiring public assistance.

In talking about the long-range cost impact of the Administration's welfare reform proposals, HEW Secretary Califano followed much the same line. A jobs program will develop better work habits in welfare families, improving the chances of family members to find jobs in the private sector. Improved family environment will also encourage young people to complete their educations. At the same time, computers will be increasingly capable of identifying cases of fraud, thus decreasing the temptation to commit fraud. Finally, if a comprehensive program begins to work there will be less need and less temptation for Congress to add to the plethora of public assistance programs.

But not everybody shares either the optimism underlying such views or the willingness to commit the sums of money required to test their validity. For many people, both in and out of Congress, the bottom line on welfare is the bottom line on the balance sheet. Faced with continual escalation of welfare costs and continual complaints about rising taxes, they will be reluctant to support welfare reform whose immediate impact is to drive up both.

WHY WAS THERE
NO MAJOR REFORM IN 1978?

Neither the White House nor Congress forgets that reforming welfare is, above all, a political action. The current program affects America's 25 million poor families and, it has been estimated, in 80 percent of the cases lifts them above the poverty line. This significant portion of the total population is acutely interested in the shape of the system. Many welfare recipients are eligible to vote. As a result, politicians will think carefully, on political grounds alone, about reforming the system in such a way as to deprive current recipients of their benefits.

Another important factor undercutting major change is that nobody knows how any reform measure would actually work. Will a given proposal mean far fewer people will qualify for benefits? Is pouring more resources into welfare a case of throwing good money after bad or will it ultimately mean that the economy will thrive and there will be fewer people on welfare? How will recipients respond? Are they mostly indolent people who welcome handouts or will they respond to incentives designed to attract them to jobs?

Most importantly, there is little support for increased spending for public assistance, at least among the Congressional leaders who can determine the fate of welfare legislation. Many of them interpret public complaints about "the welfare mess" as a mandate to cut spending.

As the Administration began work on its reform proposals, Carter himself only reluctantly accepted the inevitability of greater outlays inherent in any proposal for comprehensive change. The debate within the Administration focused on three plans. The Labor Department favored a program of guaranteed public service jobs at attractive pay levels. The Department of Health, Education and Welfare supported a uniform cash benefit, allowing for administrative simplicity and benefits based entirely on need. Still a third plan, backed by the AFL-CIO, called for the two-track system which would enable government to respond to different needs differently.

The ultimate Carter proposal had been a compromise. The jobs component was designed to attract the support of those who believe that many on welfare should work. The decision to cash out food stamps represented a move toward a comprehensive cash system. The two-track approach allowed the Administration plan to keep costs under control by avoiding raising the problem of a low benefit reduction rate and high benefit breakeven point for all welfare recipients. Fiscal relief was seen as a gesture toward the proponents of federalization of welfare. The *National Journal* concluded: "There is something here, in short, for everyone."

Despite Carter's effort to put together a broad coalition of support for his welfare plan, it ran into sharp criticism. At the outset, the *National Journal* wrote that "the cost, especially if it is seriously underestimated, could present one of the biggest barriers" to Congressional approval. This apprehension was subsequently reinforced by the first CBO review. There was sentiment on Capitol Hill that the Administration had purposely played with the figures to give an artificially low price tag to its reforms. The political damage resulting may have been greater than if the Administration had issued a higher estimate from the outset.

Even before the Administration's proposals were made public, there had been reports indicating that the President had not fully grasped the complexity of welfare reform and that he had accepted work done by HEW without understanding its implications. HEW was regarded by some on the Hill as an agency committed to a negative income tax and determined to force any president to espouse its views. As recently as 1974, HEW had developed the Income Supplement Plan (ISP). The CBO later noted that "although President Ford chose not to submit ISP to the Congress for legislative consideration, the plan represents the most comprehensive negative income tax plan developed within the executive branch." Thus, when Carter's bill was submitted, HEW was held responsible by Senators Long and Moynihan. "I believe all of us would be wise to face the fact that the overwhelming majority of the personnel who put the plan together in the Department of Health, Education and Welfare were here before President Carter came on the scene and they will be there after he is gone," said Senator Long. Senator Moynihan was even more outspoken. "The bill we received on September 12 was not drafted by the President," he charged. "It was drafted by the bureaucracy."

Concern was heightened when, in December 1977, the President said that his plan would guarantee a job to every needy family the PBJI required to work. Such a provision could be quite costly and Labor Secretary Ray Marshall was compelled immediately to explain that no such guarantee was included in the bill. As with the attack on HEW, congressmen tried to use the presidential statement to drive a wedge between Carter and his advisors. "The point is, Mr. Secretary, we want the President's statements to hold water," Representative Charles Rangel told Marshall, "so if we trust the President, why won't you?" A Marshall aide pointed out that the arbitrary limit of 1.4 million jobs had been placed in the proposal to keep cost under control. For that reason, the bill provided that those who were expected to work, but who were unable to find jobs would be treated the same as those not expected to work.

Politically, the best hope for the Carter proposal rested on the strong alliance between the White House and House Speaker Thomas "Tip" O'Neill. As he had with other pieces of priority legislation from the President, O'Neill circumvented the problems of divided committee jurisdiction by creating a special panel. The group served as a subcommittee of the standing Committees on Ways and Means, Education and Labor, and Agriculture. Speaker O'Neill's strategy was this: if the Corman Subcommittee could complete its work rapidly, the main committees would be under pressure to examine the legislation and get it to the floor of the House early enough for action in 1978. In effect, timing became the most important single consideration in the handling of welfare reform.

Because welfare is a touchy political issue, no member of

the House or Senate wanted to face the electorate in November 1978 after having voted on some provisions of the bill, but without final action having been taken. Any member could be subject to withering criticism about an individual vote that might seem to have poured more money into welfare, while being unable to justify it in terms of the entire reform package. In addition, members could expect to come under strong pressure to support the views of one interest group or another during the campaign. As a result, almost all members wanted either quick action, to be concluded well before the election, or delay until 1979. For opponents of the Carter plan, delay could be the first step toward eventual burial of the legislation.

To the considerable surprise of many in the House, reportedly including Speaker O'Neill himself, Representative Corman succeeded in clearing the bill out of his subcommittee by early February 1978. In order to do so, he had felt it necessary to give way to pressures from many members to expand the scope of the legislation and consequently to increase its cost. The Corman Subcommittee was heavily weighted toward those states with major welfare programs and a large share of the recipients, and it was almost inevitable that he would have to make progress by making concessions to recipient demands.

Corman's job was not made easier by the White House. The questionable cost estimates were a problem. The quality of the expertise and the lobbying effort mounted by HEW was dubious. In January, when the Administration was launching an effort to pass its priority legislation in 1978, it seemed as though welfare reform had been dropped. Two White House aides were quoted as acknowledging that the Administration had little hope of passing the bill in 1978. "Obviously tomorrow members are going to be saying to me 'What the hell are we doing beating our brains out?' " retorted Corman. That prompted Carter to send Corman a handwritten note, assuring him that he had "every hope and expectation" that welfare reform would pass in 1978.

Corman is reported to have put heavy pressure on O'Neill to follow through on welfare reform, once his subcommittee had cleared the legislation. Corman had acquired some leverage because of his role as chairman of the House Democratic Campaign Committee and because he had not only taken on the undesirable job that O'Neill had given him, but completed it satisfactorily.

The key committee in the House for consideration of the bill was Ways and Means. Chairman Al Ullman had opposed the Carter plan on the grounds of its high additional cost and its abandonment of traditional welfare programs, both of which he saw as making it more difficult to achieve passage. It is also clear that Ullman favored welfare programs which tend to compel recipients to work rather than merely offering them untested incentives. The House Agriculture Committee, which would have to make a decision on the cash-out of food stamps, had decided it would not act until after Ways and Means.

The time pressure was intensified by the Senate. Traditionally, Finance Committee Chairman Long will not allow full-scale consideration of welfare legislation until after it has cleared the House. House leaders were told that the Senate could not guarantee that it could act on any bill in 1978 unless it had been passed by the House before April 1. Corman's quick committee consideration had been timed to make such passage possible. Even if the bill were ready for action by the full House later in the year, there was serious doubt if members would be willing to go on record concerning a bill that the Senate would not pass. As a result, failure to act early in the House made it increasingly unlikely that any action would be taken in 1978.

O'Neill, responding to pressure from Corman, tried to get Ullman to give priority consideration to welfare reform. But Ullman responded that the President had asked for action on tax reform, an attractive bill in an election year. Ullman said he would only delay tax reform and give welfare reform early consideration if asked to do so by the White House. Such a request was never made.

On the Senate side, Chairman Long was obviously in no hurry to deal with the Carter plan or a House version of it. He believed that the PBJI would make more people dependent on welfare benefits and, unless the Administration were able to convince him that the plan would actually remove people from the welfare rolls, he would be unlikely to show any sympathy toward it. His only willingness to compromise was his offer to test the PBJI in specific areas in return for tests of his own workfare concepts.

Senator Moynihan, whose Public Assistance Subcommittee is under the jurisdiction of Long's Finance Committee, began hearings so that the Senate could not be accused of causing the delay on 1978 action. Moynihan's criticisms of the bill were almost diametrically opposed to Long's. He felt that many provisions were not sufficiently generous. Although Moynihan's ultimate influence will be limited by Long's dominant role, he has an advantage in the debate that appears to distinguish him from all other members of Congress: he possesses a significant expertise on the subject and a grasp of the details. In fact, it had become clear during the Corman Subcommittee's work, that few of its members fully understood the provisions under consideration. As a result, discussions of the bill became the preserve of staff aides. In any future Senate-House conference on a welfare reform bill, Moynihan's expertise plus his standing could be of prime importance.

A complicating factor in the Senate was the joint referral of the bill to the Finance and Human Resources Committees. Senator Long maintained that Human Resources could deal only with the jobs part of the PBJI. He was obviously concerned that the Human Resources Committee would adopt a more liberal bill than might come out of the Finance Committee. Human Resources, chaired by Senator Harrison Williams of New Jersey, also scheduled early hearings on the Carter plan.

"Welfare reform will not come about in this nation unless a broad coalition of interest can be mustered around a set of general principles and a series of specific propositions," Senator Moynihan had told the Corman Subcommittee. "There are already ample warnings that the Administration's proposals are not going to attract the necessary coalition of support, at least in part because many liberal-minded individuals and groups find them wanting."

Moynihan's finding seems to have been borne out. And, unlike the debate over the Nixon Family Assistance Plan, where liberal groups were united in asking for more and, as a result, actually helped the Administration, there was no such cohesive force in Congress. Carter had alienated a large number of liberal groups without making significant compensating gains among more conservative members of Congress. In effect, the changes that the Corman Subcommittee made in the original legislation represented an effort to regain liberal support for comprehensive reform.

By contrast, the Ullman alternative was intended to appeal to those who found fault with the Carter plan, especially on the grounds that it would bring too sharp an increase in welfare spending. In effect, the Ways and Means Chairman attempted to build a more conservative coalition.

By March 1978, the White House recognized that, despite its success in the Corman Subcommittee, it had little hope of securing passage of a comprehensive reform measure in the 95th Congress. That month, Carter met with Corman, Ullman, Long and Moynihan to signal his willingness to pull back from his bill. White House officials reported that Carter still wanted the PBJI, but recognized that, if the Administration took an all-or-nothing approach, it would probably get nothing. "He sees the need for some compromise," one of his aides said.

Carter's shift set the stage for an effort to develop a compromise bill that might embody provisions of the Carter-Corman proposals and of the alternatives proposed in the Baker-Bellmon and Ullman bills. In mid-May, Moynihan and Ullman met with representatives of a group calling itself the New Coalition who offered to attempt to draw up an acceptable compromise. The New Coalition was composed of some of the groups which had been most deeply involved in the reform debate and which have the greatest stake in welfare legislation: the National Governor's Association (the permanent organization of the National Governors Conference), the National Conference of State Legislatures, the National Association of Counties, the National League of Cities and the U.S. Conference of Mayors. The two Congressional leaders indicated that they would try to speed action in their own committees if the New Coalition could produce an acceptable bill in short order.

By June 7, the New Coalition was ready to present its proposal to a meeting of House leaders, Presidential advisor Stuart Eizenstat, HEW Secretary Califano, and Labor Secretary

Marshall. Massachusetts Governor Michael Dukakis represented the New Coalition.

Although the draft compromise would have established a minimum national benefit level at 65 percent of the poverty line, it represented an incremental rather han a comprehensive approach to welfare reform. The AFDC, SSI and food stamp programs would have remained intact, but greater administrative uniformity among them would have been imposed. This streamlining would have included the coordination of benefit reduction rates among several income maintenance programs. The AFDC program for two-parent families would have been mandated in all states.

The jobs portion of the package would have provided an additional 650,000 slots for employment and training under CETA, and proponents suggested that at least 100,000 CETA jobs under Titles II and VI would also be made available to welfare recipients. The earned income tax credit would have been expanded as an incentive to private-sector employment. In addition, demonstration projects using job vouchers were proposed.

Not surprisingly, given the composition of the New Coalition, the compromise provided for state or state-local administration of AFDC and for an increased Federal match for both the minimum benefit payments and supplements up to the poverty line.

The New Coalition proposal appeared to accept many of Ullman's suggestions. (See Appendix I for a comparison of its key provisions with those of the other bills.) Ullman himself had accepted the concept of a national minimum benefit, so that one of the most important elements of the PBJI had survived.

At the June 7 meeting, a consensus emerged indicating that both Congressional leaders and the Administration could support such a package. However, Ullman insisted that, when the compromise was drafted as legislation, its added cost to current welfare programs would have to be less than $10 billion.

In late June, as the bill was being developed, it became clear that Ullman's limit could not be maintained without additional cutbacks in the compromise. House staff members projected a cost for the New Coalition's compromise that might go as high as $14 billion above the cost of the present programs. Some participants in the New Coalition said they could not agree to any further reductions in the scope of reform.

At this point, the House leadership was faced with the prospect of continued protracted negotiations to develop an acceptable compromise at an acceptable cost. At the same time, Congress was showing increased unwillingness to expand Federal spending in the wake of the June 6 California referendum on Proposition 13 which mandated a sharp reduction in that state's property taxes. The overwhelming vote in favor of Proposition 13 was seen in Washington as an indication of a national taxpayers' revolt against increased government spending. And surveys continued to show that many people believed that welfare was the prime target for cost-cutting.

Time was running out. Senate leaders told House Speaker O'Neill that it was now most unlikely that a major reform bill could be brought before the Senate in 1978. House members remained reluctant to pass any reform legislation without the assurance that the Senate would also act. "All during the negotiations there's been a nagging question: Is it realistic to expect the Senate to act?" said Corman. "The Speaker said no ... so there is no point in further negotiations."

Major welfare reform in 1978 was dead. The prospect remained for only relatively minor changes that would be the object of little or no controversy. Ullman and Moynihan aides suggested that these measures might include reauthorization of CETA, expansion of the EITC, incentives for private-sector employers to hire welfare recipients, some improvements in the AFDC program and expanded fiscal relief for the states. Senator Long was reported to be willing to go along with most of these proposals. As for the Carter Administration, the White House said that it would press for action on a modified version of the New Coalition proposal in 1979.

The most important single factor in the demise of welfare reform legislation in 1978 was the unwillingness of many in

Congress to vote additional funds for public assistance even if the welfare system were improved. Carter had been forced to admit that it was impossible to keep his campaign promise to make the system more efficient and equitable at no added cost.

To many in Washington, 1978 had appeared to be the year of opportunity if there were to be any major restructuring of the program during the Carter Administration. But the complexity of the proposals under consideration, many of which were simply not understood by most people in Congress, coupled with increasing cost consciousness caused the opportunity to vanish.

Yet the welfare debate of 1978 had served a purpose. Whenever major reform would again come before Congress, whether in 1979 or after the next Presidential election, the key issues would have been defined during the debate engendered by the PBJI.

APPENDIX I

COMPARISON OF POSITIONS
ON
WELFARE REFORM ISSUES

MAJOR PROVISIONS OF CURRENT WELFARE REFORM BILLS

Present Law	Carter Proposal	Corman Proposal	Ullman Proposal	Baker-Bellmon Proposal	New Coalition Proposal
COVERAGE Categorical; AFDC, SSI, food stamps.	Universal; food stamps cashed out; two-tier ETW and NETW	Universal; food stamps kept as option; two-tier	Categorical; AFDC, SSI (food stamps cashed out), food stamps, AFDC-UP in all states	Categorical; AFDC, SSI (optional food stamp cashout), food stamps, AFDC-UP in all states	Categorical; AFDC, SSI (food stamps cashed out), food stamps, AFDC-UP in all states
Filing unit: Nuclear or sub-nuclear family	Nuclear family; separate status for ABD and AFDC living with relatives	Same as Carter, but singles under 25 must file with parents	AFDC: nuclear family SSI: individuals, couples Food stamps: all persons living together	Nuclear family; separate status for ABD	No position
ELIGIBILITY					
Current need	6-month retrospective income accounting; no Federal tax on benefits	1-month retrospective income accounting; tax on cash assistance	1-month retrospective; tax recoupment of "excess" benefits	State option: current need or 1-month retrospective; recoupment	State option: current need of 1-month retrospective
BENEFITS (annual in 1978 dollars)					
States determine, with range from $2760 to $6276 for family of 4	$4200 for family of 4; $2300 lower tier; $2500 single ABD; $1100 single; benefits increase with family size up to 7	Same as Carter, but no limit on family size	$4200 for family of 4. Max. AFDC is 30% of state median income less food stamps. AFDC same for all family sizes	AFDC and food stamps at 55% of 1981 poverty line, 60% of 1982 poverty line, 65% of 1985 poverty line (60% of 1978 poverty line was $3720)	AFDC and food stamps at 65% of poverty line (65% of 1978 poverty line was $4030)
Not indexed in line with cost of living.	Not indexed, but may be changed	Indexed	Indexed	Indexed	Indexed
Earned income disregard is $30/mo. plus one-third income plus actual work expenses	NETW: EID is 50% plus $150 child care up to $300/mo. ETW: EID $317/mo. plus 50%	Same as Carter	EID is $30/mo. plus one-third income, plus $100 per child up to $300/mo.	EID is $60/mo. plus one-third income, plus work expenses up to $60/mo. plus $100 per child up to $300/mo.	EID is $60/mo. plus 40% income plus $150 child care up to $300/mo.
Benefit reduction rate is 67% AFDC, 30% food stamps	Basic rate 50%; max. allowed with state supplement ETW 52%, NETW 70% (food stamps cashed out)	Basic rate 50%; max. allowed with state supplement 70%; rate for marginal food stamp program 30%	Basic rate 67% for single parent AFDC, 60% for 2-parent AFDC; no limit on state rate for supplement; food stamps 20%-40%	Same as present law	Basic rate AFDC 60%; max. allowed with state supplement. Social Security and Federal income tax: 50-70% in income range $5000-$7000, 80% in income range $7000-$10,000

Present Law	Carter Proposal	Corman Proposal	Ullman Proposal	Baker-Bellmon Proposal	New Coalition Proposal
EARNED INCOME TAX CREDIT					
10% to $4000, then 10% phaseout	10% to $4000, then 5% to poverty line, then 10% phaseout; reverse withholding	12% to $4200 (indexed) then 6% phaseout; reverse withholding	20% to $5000, then flat to $7500, then 13% reverse withholding	15% to poverty line, then 20% phaseout; reverse withholding	20% to min. wage, then 20% phaseout; reverse withholding
WORK REQUIREMENT					
All able-bodied adults to participate in WIN and accept employment with some exceptions	All able-bodied adults to accept employment offered through Labor Dept; some exceptions. Single parent with child under 7 must work part-time	Same as Carter	Basically same as present law	Basically same as present law	Basically same as present law
ADMINISTRATION					
All except SSI by states, localities	Federal, but states could handle intake	Federal, but state option to handle cash program	State, except for SSI; not localities	State, except for SSI; not localities unless Federal funding cut	State, but state may choose to share administration with localities
MANDATED STATE SPENDING/FISCAL RELIEF FROM PRESENT STATE SPENDING					
States pay 17% to 50% AFDC; no mandated share; states pay 50% of administration	States to pay 10% of Federal basic amount; 90% of current in first year, 75% in 2nd; 65% in 3rd; 0% of administration	Same as Carter	States to pay 85% of 1977 single parent AFDC forever; after delay, must pay $200/mo. to AFDC-UP; 50% of administration; 50% of errors.	States to pay 10% - 20% depending on errors; 50% of administration	States to pay 10% AFDC, 50% of administration
States and localities pay $16.3 billion in fiscal 1978	$3.36 billion in fiscal 1982 as relief to states	$2.21 billion in fiscal 1982 as relief to states	$1 to $2 billion in fiscal 1982 as relief to states	$3.05 billion in fiscal 1982 as relief to states	$1.5-$2.5 billion in fiscal 1982 as relief to states
FEDERAL MATCHING OF STATE BENEFIT SUPPLEMENTS					
AFDC ranges from 50% to 83%	75% to $4714; 25% to poverty line	75% to $4714; 25% to higher of poverty line or sum of AFDC and food stamps	Difference between 85% of 1977 state share and Federal benefit but 0% for state supplements	State supplement at state expense	65% to poverty line or current level for single parent families; 65% up to 80% of poverty line for two-parent families

	Present Law	Carter Proposal	Corman Proposal	Ullman Proposal	Baker-Bellmon Proposal	New Coalition Proposal
JOB CREATION: PRIVATE SECTOR	Tax credit for hiring WIN registrants	Not provided	Not provided	Expands on tax credit for new jobs for WIN registrants	Employer can choose $1 per hour voucher or $1 per hour job credit for one year for AFDC, long-term unemployed, former CETA workers	Job creation — 5 yr. demonstration project on job vouchers
JOB CREATION: PUBLIC SECTOR	CETA now provides 725,000 slots; WIN 200,000 slots	CETA to provide 1.4 million slots, including 300,000 part-time; minimum wage; abolish WIN	Same as Carter except equal pay for equal work as between CETA and other employees	WIN to provide 524,000 new slots; states to control WIN	Would gradually reduce CETA; CETA jobs for long-term unemployed, with 50% remaining slots to AFDC; CETA 250,000 in fiscal 1983; states to control WIN; WIN to received added funds	650,000 additional CETA jobs, minimum wage
NET ADDITIONAL FEDERAL COST (in fiscal year 1982)	Federal costs are $36.9 billion in fiscal 1978	$19.14 billion added (assuming indexing)	$20.22 billion added	$7.5 to $9 billion added	$9.3 billion added	$10-$14 billion added

ABBREVIATIONS

AFDC   Aid to Families with Dependent Children
AFDC-UP   Aid to Families with Dependent Children-Unemployed Parent
ETW   Expected to work
NETW   Not expected to work
ABD   Aged, blind or disabled

SSI   Supplemental Security Income
EID   Earned income disregard
CETA   Comprehensive Employment and Training Act
WIN   Work incentive program

Note: This table does not cover all proposed legislative changes and, of necessity, provisions are summarized. Fuller explanation in text.

POSITIONS OF KEY GROUPS ON MAJOR PROVISIONS OF CURRENT WELFARE REFORM BILLS

	Nat'l Governors Assn.	AFL-CIO	APWA	NASW	ACU
COVERAGE					
	Universal, food stamps cashed out, opposed to two-tier	Universal, food stamps, three-track	Universal, food stamps cashed out	Universal, food stamps cashed out; opposed to two-tier	State systems, not universal, food stamps
	N.p. on filing unit	N.p. on filing suit	N.p. on filing unit	Opposes Corman inclusion of 18-25 year olds in basic family	Opposes extended family concept, seen to be in Carter
ELIGIBILITY					
	Favors new rules, not specific	Opposes Carter, prefers current need	N.p.	Prefers Corman, but also wants administrative delay eliminated	Opposes Carter, prefers both prospective and retrospective accounting
BENEFITS					
	$4200 level is acceptable	$4200 inadequate; prefers poverty level	$4200 inadequate	$4200 inadequate; prefers poverty level	Assistance should only be in-kind in line with need
	EID should be continued or increased	EID too low in Carter for child-care	N.p.	EID too low in Carter for child-care	EID may be too high based on definition of what is income
	Benefit reduction rate no more than 70%; up to states	N.p.	N.p.	States with high benefit reduction rate should be required to provide high supplements	Does not favor financial work incentive; work requirement preferred
EARNED INCOME TAX CREDIT					
	N.p.	Should be geared to family size; targeted on working poor; Carter is weak on this	N.p.	Should not be limited by family size; eligibility in Carter-Corman too narrow	Carter depends on impact of general tax reform; phaseout may be too high

Nat'l Governors Assn.	AFL-CIO	APWA	NASW	ACU
WORK REQUIREMENT				
Generally accepts Corman; no mandatory government work	Opposes Carter-Corman; says it would create second-class work force	Accepts Carter; wants employable recipients to be required to take job, training	Carter-Corman: unnecessary and stigmatizing	Present rules are preferable to Carter; favors stringent work requirement
ADMINISTRATION				
State; block grants preferred	State-Federal with job protection for state employees	State and local	Either Federal or state; prefers Federal	States with broad discretion; block grants
MANDATED STATE SPENDING/FISCAL RELIEF FROM PRESENT STATE SPENDING				
Not specific, but willing to continue financial participation in social services	N.p.	N.p.	States should be required to maintain 100% of current effort	N.p.
Accepts Carter on fiscal relief; prefers federalization of welfare costs	Carter fiscal relief may be illusory as states move to cover those excluded from benefits	Generally favors Carter, but questions actual amount	N.p.	Carter fiscal relief likely to be distributed among states inequitably
FEDERAL MATCHING OF STATE BENEFIT SUPPLEMENTS				
N.p., but favors block grants	Supplementation should be required, not merely encouraged	Carter rules could limit state flexibility on supplements	N.p.	States with broad discretion
JOB CREATION: PRIVATE SECTOR				
Prefers incentives to welfare recipients rather than to employers	Massive effort called for, not specific	N.p.	N.p.	Stimulation of private sector to create jobs as part of economic policy
JOB CREATION: PUBLIC SECTOR				
Supports Carter-Corman	Carter provides insufficient number of jobs; program opposed unless at prevailing wage	Similar to AFL-CIO	Similar to AFL-CIO; wants more employment support services	Public employment creates jobs for which there is no need; may not be practicable

111

Nat'l Governors Assn.	AFL-CIO	APWA	NASW	ACU
COST				
N.p.	Willing to accept greater increases than in Carter in order to increase wage, benefit levels	N.p.	N.p.	Costs can be reduced by cutting cash payment for employable recipients

ABBREVIATIONS

APWA	American Public Welfare Association
NASW	National Association of Social Workers
ACU	American Conservative Union
N.p.	No position
EID	Earned income disregard

Note: This table does not cover all proposed legislative changes nor all of the positions taken by these groups, and, of necessity, positions are summarized. They are derived from Congressional testimony and interviews and, in the case of the National Governors Association, from the results of a questionnaire sent to all governors. A fuller explanation of positions is in the text and copies of statements may be obtained directly from the organizations, whose addresses are in the Directory. Positions of groups in this table may not be representative of positions of similar groups. No welfare client group presented a sufficiently comprehensive position to be included in this table, but the NASW position is generally representative of many client views. The emphasis that the various groups place on issues in the welfare reform debate may be inferred from those issues on which they take no position.

APPENDIX II

DIRECTORY OF ORGANIZATIONS CONCERNED WITH WELFARE POLICY

NOTE: The following is a list of governmental and nongovern-
mental organizations concerned with the development of
national welfare policy. Not all policy-oriented organizations are
listed, but the directory includes a wide variety of those which
have played leading roles in the welfare debate. Also included
are the names of people involved in the development of policy
positions on the operating staff level and in the academic world.

GOVERNMENT: EXECUTIVE BRANCH

Department of Health, Education and Welfare
330 Independence Avenue, S.W.
Washington, DC 20201

Joseph A. Califano, Jr., *Secretary*	202/245-7000
Henry Aaron, *Assistant Secretary, Planning and Evaluation*	202/245-1858
Michael C. Barth, *Deputy Assistant Secretary, Income Security Policy*	202/245-6591
John Todd, *Director, Analysis*	202/245-6141
Thomas Ault, *Director, Planning*	202/245-7155
Larry Orr, *Director, Research*	202/245-6353
Dan Marcus, *Deputy General Counsel*	202/245-6733
Ann Sobel, *State-local Government Coordinator*	202/245-6141
Dorothy Stimpson, *State-local Government Coordinator*	202/245-1865
Dave Betson, *Staff Economist*	202/245-6619
Barry Van Lare, *Director, Office of Family Assistance*	202/245-0413
Paul Gayer, *Liaison with Labor Department*	202/245-6443
Dick Michael, *Cost Specialist*	202/245-7155

Department of Labor
200 Constitution Avenue, N.W.
Washington, DC 20201

F. Ray Marshall, *Secretary*	202/523-8271
Jodie T. Allen, *Special Assistant, Welfare Reform*	202/523-9184
Arnold Packer, *Assistant Secretary, Policy, Evaluation & Research*	202/523-6181
Gary Reed, *Director, Office of Income Maintenance*	202/523-6007

Department of Agriculture
14th Street & Independence Avenue, S.W.
Washington, DC 20250

Carol Tucker Foreman, *Assistant Secretary, Food and Consumer Services*	202/447-4623

Executive Office of the President
The White House Office   202/456-1414
1600 Pennsylvania Avenue, N.W.
Washington, DC 20500

Stuart Eizenstat, *Assistant to the President for Domestic Affairs & Policy*	202/456-6515
Bertram Carp, *Deputy Director, Domestic Council*	202/456-2562

Office of Management and Budget
Executive Office Building
Washington, DC 20502

Suzanne Woolsey, *Associate Director, Human Resources*	202/395-4844

Council of Economic Advisors
Executive Office Building
Washington, DC 20406

William Spring, *Senior Staff Economist*	202/395-5040

114

GOVERNMENT: CONGRESS

House Committee on Ways and Means   202/225-3625
  Rep. Al Ullman, *Chairman*
  Rep. Barber B. Conable, *Ranking Minority Member*
  Wendell Primas, *Economist*

Subcommittee on Public Assistance   202/225-1025
  Rep. James C. Corman, *Chairman*
  Kenneth Bowler, *Professional Staff Member*   202/225-1076
  Florence Prioleau, *Professional Staff Member*   202/225-1025

House Committee on Education and Labor   202/225-4527
  Rep. Carl D. Perkins, *Chairman*
  Rep. Albert H. Quie, *Ranking Minority Member*
  Donald Baker, *Chief Clerk*

Subcommittee on Employment Opportunities   202/225-1927
  Rep. Augustus F. Hawkins, *Chairman*
  Susan Grayson, *Staff Director*

House Committee on Agriculture   202/225-2171
  Rep. Thomas S. Foley, *Chairman*
  Rep. William C. Wampler, *Ranking Minority Member*
  Sharon Armann, *Staff Assistant*

House Budget Committee   202/225-7200
  Rep. Robert N. Giaimo, *Chairman*
  Alair A. Townsend, *Senior Analyst*

Subcommittee on Distributive Impacts of Budget and Economic Policies   202/225-4446
  Rep. Donald Fraser, *Chairman*
  Jane Shelburne, *Professional Staff Member*

Subcommittee on State and Local Government   202/225-6615
  Rep. Elizabeth Holtzman, *Chairman*
  Stanley Collendar, *Professional Staff Member*

NOTE: All House of Representatives addresses are
      Washington, DC 20515

Senate Finance Committee   202/224-4515
  Sen. Russell Long, *Chairman*
  Sen. Carl T. Curtis, *Ranking Minority Member*
  Michael Stern, *Staff Director*

Subcommittee on Public Assistance   202/224-9550
  Sen. Daniel Patrick Moynihan, *Chairman*
  William R. Galvin, *Professional Staff Member*

Senate Committee on Human Resources   202/224-5375
  Sen. Harrison A. Williams, *Chairman*
  Sen. Jacob K. Javits, *Ranking Minority
    Member*
  J. Martin Jenson, *Professional Staff Member*   202/244-3656

Senate Agriculture Committee   202/224-2035
  Sen. Herman Talmadge, *Chairman*
  Sen. Robert Dole, *Ranking Minority Member*

Subcommittee on Nutrition   202/224-7326
  Sen. George McGovern, *Chairman*
  Marshall L. Martz, *Special Counsel*
  Sen. Howard H. Baker, *Senate Minority
    Leader*   202/224-4944
  Rob Mosbacher, *Legislative Assistant*
  Sen. Harry L. Bellmon   202/224-5754
  Doug Jackson, *Chief Legislative Assistant*
  Sen. Abraham A. Ribicoff   202/224-2823
  Susan Irving, *Staff Assistant*

NOTE: All U.S. Senate addresses are
      Washington, DC 20510

Joint Economic Committee   202/224-5171
  Room G-133
  Dirksen Senate Office Building
  Washington, DC 20510

  Rep. Richard Bolling
  Sen. Lloyd Bentsen
  John Stark, *Executive Director*
  George Krumbhaar, Jr., *Minority Counsel*

116

Advisory Commission on Intergovernmental Relations   202/633-7065
726 Jackson Place, N.W.
Washington, DC 20575

Richard Gabler, *Senior Analyst*

Congressional Budget Office
Room 3540, House Annex 2
Second and D Streets, S.W.
Washington, DC 20515

Robert D. Reischauer, *Assistant Director*   202/225-1264
William Fisher, *Professional Staff Member*   202/225-1264
William Hoegland, *Professional Staff Member*   202/225-1491
John Korbel, *Professional Staff Member*   202/225-1260
Stanley Wallack, *Professional Staff Member*   202/225-4655

General Accounting Office
Task Force on Alternative Income Distribution   202/523-9009
    Systems
Room N 1658
200 Constitution Avenue, N.W.
Washington, DC 20210

John Moundalexis, *Assistant Director*
John Carney, *Professional Staff Member*
Dan Bryer, *Professional Staff Member*

NONGOVERNMENTAL ORGANIZATIONS

American Conservative Union   202/546-6555
422 First Street, S.E.
Washington, DC 20003

Rep. Bill Goodling, *Chairman/Welfare Task*   202/225-5836
Force
Robert B. Carleson, *Advisor on Welfare*
Reform
James Roberts, *Executive Director*

Related Group:
Heritage Foundation   202/546-4400
513 C Street, N.E.
Washington, DC 20002

American Enterprise Institute   202/862-5800
1150 17th Street, N.W. — Suite 1200
Washington, DC 20036

Robert B. Helms, *Director, Center for Health*
Studies

AFL-CIO   202/637-5000
815 16th Street, N.W.
Washington, DC 20006

Bert Seidman, *Director, Social Security*   202/637-5200
Department
Mary Logan, *Assistant Director, Social*   202/637-5208
Security Department

American Federation of State, County and   202/452-4800
Municipal Employees
1625 L Street, N.W.
Washington, DC 20036

Robert McGarrah, *Public Policy Counsel*   202/452-4937

American Public Welfare Association   202/833-9250
1155 16th Street, N.W.
Washington, DC 20036

Steven Minter, *President*
Edward Weaver, *Executive Director*
John Horejsi, *Staff Assistant*

Related groups:

National Council of Local Public Welfare Adminstrators

Miles J. Wangensteen, *Chairman*

National Council of State Public Welfare Administrators

John J. Affleck, *Chairman*

Brookings Institution   202/797-6000
1775 Massachusetts Avenue, N.W.
Washington, DC 20036

Joseph A. Pechman, *Director of Economics*
Richard Nathan, *Senior Fellow*
Arthur M. Okun, *Senior Fellow*
John L. Palmer, *Senior Fellow*
Gilbert Steiner, *Senior Fellow*

Center on Social Welfare Policy and Law   212/679-3709
95 Madison Avenue
New York, NY 10016

Adele Blong, *Associate Director*

Chamber of Commerce of the United States   202/659-6170
Economic Security, Education and Manpower
   Section
1615 H Street, N.W.
Washington, DC 20062

Robert F. Erburu, *Chairman, Panel on Welfare
   Reform Proposals*   213/486-3814

Michael J. Romig, *Panel Executive, Panel on
Welfare Reform Proposals*   202/659-6106
Linda S. McMahon, *Associate Director, Social
Insurance and Welfare*   202/659-6106
Dorothy Tella, *Staff Executive, Council on
Trends and Perspective*   202/659-6163

Child Welfare League   202/833-2850
1346 Connecticut Avenue, N.W.
Washington, DC 20036

William Pierce, *Assistant Executive Director*

Candace Mueller, *Director of the Hecht
Institute*

The Council of State Governments   212/221-3630
1500 Broadway
New York, NY 10036

Alan V. Sokolow, *Director, Eastern Regional
Office*
Jonathan Caciala, *Associate Director of
State Service*

Headquarters Office: 606/252-2291
Iron Works Pike
Lexington, KY 40511

Council on National Priorities and Resources 202/293-9114
1620 I Street, N.W.
Washington, DC 20007

Reuben McCornack, *Director*

Council on Social Work Education   212/OX 7-0467
345 East 46th Street
New York, NY 10017

James R. Dumpson, *Chairman*
Richard Lodge, *Executive Director*

CONEG (Coalition of Northeast Governors)   212/223-1750
Research Center
135 West 50th Street
New York, NY 10020

David Tobis, *Research Associate*

Family Service Association   202/785-2438
1819 H Street, N.W.
Washington, DC 20006

Keith W. Daugherty, *General Director*
Pat Langley, *Washington Representative*   202/659-8732

Food Research and Action Center   202/452-8250
2011 I Street, N.W. — Suite 700
Washington, DC 20006

Ronald Pollack, *Director*

The Institute for Socioeconomic Studies   914/428-7400
Airport Road
White Plains, NY 10604

Leonard M. Greene, *President*

League of Women Voters   202/296-1770
1730 M Street, N.W.
Washington, DC 20036

Regina O'Leary, *Chairman, Income Assistance*
Nan Waterman, *Chairman, Human Resources*

Mathematica Policy Research, Inc.   609/799-2600
Princeton, NJ 08540·

Kenneth Kehrer, *Vice President & Director of
Survey Division*

NAACP   212/245-2100
1790 Broadway
New York, NY 10019

Benjamin L. Hooks, *Executive Director*

Washington Bureau   202/638-2269
722 15th Street, N.W.
Washington, DC 20005

Clarence Mitchell, *Director, Washington Bureau*

National Association of Counties   202/785-9577
1735 New York Avenue, N.W.
Washington, DC 20006

Alice Ann Fristchler, *Associate Director*
Pat Johnson, *Consultant*

National Association of Social Workers   202/628-6800
1425 H Street, N.W.
Washington, DC 20005

Al Gonzalez, *Staff Associate for Legislation*

National Association of State Budget Officers   202/624-5380
444 North Capitol Street
Washington, DC 20001

Raymond Long, *Executive Director*

National Conference on Social Welfare   202/785-0817
919 18th Street, N.W.
Washington, DC 20006

Dorothy Hurwitz, *Director, Washington Office*

New York Office: 212/673-5660
225 Park Avenue South
New York, NY 10003

Margaret Berry, *Executive Director*

National Conference of State Legislatures   202/624-5400
444 North Capitol Street
Washington, DC 20001

Dick Merritt, *Staff Director for Human Resources*

National Council of Churches   202/544-2350
110 Maryland Avenue, N.E.
Washington, DC 20002

James A. Hamilton, *Director Washington Office*

National Council of Jewish Women   202/296-2588
1346 Connecticut Avenue, N.W.
Washington, DC 20036

Olya Margolin, *Washington Representative*

National Council of La Raza   202/659-1251
1725 I Street, N.W.
Washington, DC 20006

Raul Yzaguirre, *National Director*

National Governors Association   202/624-5300
444 North Capitol Street
Washington, DC 20001

Peter O'Donnell, *Staff Associate, Division of Human Resources*
Joan Wills, *Staff Director, Employment and Vocational Training Programs*

Scott Bunton, *Staff Director, Committee on
Human Resources*

National League of Cities — U.S. Conference   202/293-7300
of Mayors
1620 I Street, N.W.
Washington, DC 20006

Carol Kocheisen, *Senior Legislative Counsel*   202/293-7380
Joan Miller, *Consultant*   202/293-7580
Dorothy Brody, *Associate Director*   202/293-7572

National Organization for Women (NOW)   202/347-2279
425 13th Street, N.W.
Washington, DC 20004

Margaret Mason, *Welfare Rights Aide*

National Urban Coalition   202/331-2400
1201 Connecticut Avenue, N.W.
Washington, DC 20036

Sarah Austin, *Executive Vice President*

National Urban League   212/644-6500
500 East 62nd Street
New York, NY 10021

Vernon E. Jordan, Jr., *Executive Director*

Washington Bureau   202/393-4332
425 13th Street, N.W.
Washington, DC 20004

Ronald Brown, *Director*

National Women's Political Caucus   202/347-4456
1411 K Street, N.W.
Washington, DC 20005

Lupe Auguiano, *Chairman, Welfare Task Force*

Regional Plan Association   212/682-7750
235 East 45th Street
New York, NY 10017

John P. Keith, *President*
Joseph Thomas, *Senior Fellow*

Stanford Research Institute   415/326-6200
Menlo Park, CA 94025

Robert G. Spiegelman, *Director, Center for
the Study of Welfare Policy*

United Auto Workers (UAW)   202/296-7484
1125 15th Street, N.W.
Washington, DC 20005

Howard G. Pastor, *Director of Legislation*

U.S. Catholic Conference   202/659-6600
1312 Massachusetts Avenue, N.W.
Washington, DC 20002

Rev. Msgr. Francis J. Lally, *Secretary,
Department of Social Development and World
Peace*
Barbara Stolz, *Coordinator for Social
Domestic Issues*

U.S. Conference of Mayors
See National League of Cities

Urban Institute   202/223-1950
2100 M Street, N.W.
Washington, DC 20037

Robert Harris, *Senior Vice President*
Lee Bawden, *Professional Staff Member*
Wayne Hoffman, *Professional Staff Member*

ACADEMIC INSTITUTIONS

Boston College   617/969-0100
Social Welfare Regional Research Institute   x 4070
Chestnut Hill, MA 02167

Professor Barry Bluestone

Brandeis University   617/647-2936
Heller Graduate School
Waltham, MA 02154

Professor Leonard J. Hausman
Professor Barry L. Friedman

Catholic University   202/635-5458
School of Social Work
620 Michigan Avenue, N.E.
Washington, DC 20064

Alvin L. Schorr, *Visiting Professor*

Columbia University   212/280-3681
Department of Economics
1022 International Affairs Building
New York, NY 10027

Professor Harold Watts
Professor C. Lowell Harriss

School of Social Work   212/280-5188
622 West 113th Street
New York, NY 10025

Dean Mitchell I. Ginsberg
Professor Richard A. Cloward

Harvard University
Cambridge, MA 02138

Professor Martin S. Feldstein, *Department of*   617/495-2144
Economics

Professor Lee Rainwater, *Sociology*
   Department
617/495-3825

Massachusetts Institute of Technology
Cambridge, MA 02138
617/253-1000

Professor Lester Thurow, *Economics Department*
Professor Martin Rein, *Urban Studies*

New York University
Department of Economics
Tisch Hall - Fifth Floor
40 W. Fourth Street
New York, NY 10003
212/598-7874

Professor Bruno Stein

Stanford University
Hoover Institution
Stanford, CA 94305
415/497-3373

Professor Milton Friedman
Professor Martin Anderson
415/497-0580
415/497-4742

State University of New York (Albany)
Graduate School of Public Affairs
Albany, NY 12222
518/457-3300

Professor Irene Lurie

University of Chicago
Center for the Study of Welfare Policy
5801 South Ellis Avenue
Chicago, IL 60637
312/753-4606

Professor Thomas C.W. Joe

University of Massachusetts/Amherst
Sociology Department
Amherst, MA 01002
413/545-3416

127

Professor Peter H. Rossi

University of Michigan
The Institute for Social Research   313/764-8363
Ann Arbor, MI 48106

F. Thomas Juster, *Director*
James Wessel, *Assistant Director*

University of Pennsylvania
Department of Social Welfare   215/243-5511
3701 Locust Walk
Philadelphia, PA 19104

Professor June Axinn

George Washington University
Center for Social Policy Studies   202/833-2530
1819 H Street, N.W.
Washington, DC 20006

Professor Sar A. Levitan

University of Wisconsin
Institute for Research on Poverty   608/262-6358
3412 Social Science Building
Madison WI 53706

Irwin Garfinkel, *Director*
Felicity Skidmore, *Workshop Coordinator*
John H. Bishop, *Project Associate*

Also:
Professor Robert Lampman, *Department of*
   Economics   608/262-8829
Professor Robert H. Haveman, *Department of*
   Economics   608/263-7389
Professor Eugene Smolensky, *Department of*
   Economics   608/263-7397

Professor Sheldon Danziger, *Department of Economics*   608/263-3660
Joel F. Handler, *Professor of Law*   608/262-6358

Yale University
Department of Economics   203/436-8330
New Haven, CT 06520

Professor James Tobin

INDEX

130

Veterans' pensions, 6

War on Poverty, 2, 70
Ways and Means Committee, House,
61, 100; cost estimates of Ullman
proposal, 93
Weinberger, Caspar W., 4
Welfare administration, 7-8, 69;
APWA position, 65, 68; in Corman
proposal, 66; National Governors
Conference survey on, 67-68; under
PBJI, 65-66; in Ullman proposal, 67
Welfare, federal/state funding of, 7-
8; in Baker-Bellmon proposal, 61-62;
in Corman proposal, 60; under PBJI,
58-60; in Ullman proposal, 61
Welfare fraud, 7
Welfare reform, approaches to:

categorical assistance, 29; comprehensive, 9-10, 13, 16-17, 33; consolidated cash assistance, 29; incremental, 9-10, 14-17, 34; track
system (work/welfare approach), 11,
29
Wellhead tax, 74, 88
Western Center on Law and Poverty,
42
Wisconsin, University of. *See* Institute
for Research on Poverty
Work Incentive Program (WIN), 7, 88;
in Baker-Bellmon proposal, 23; in
Ullman proposal, 21-22
Workmen's compensation, 5
Wurf, Jerry, 24

Young, Ned L., 46